W9-CMJ-234

I. A. Richards' Theory of Literature

YALE INSTITUTION FOR
SOCIAL AND POLICY STUDIES

PN
81
.R53
S3
1969

I. A. Richards'
Theory of Literature

Jerome P. Schiller

YALE UNIVERSITY PRESS
NEW HAVEN AND LONDON
1969

SALEM COLLEGE LIBRARY
WINSTON-SALEM, N. C.

Published with assistance from the foundation
established in memory of Amasa Stone Mather
of the Class of 1907, Yale College
Copyright © 1969 by Yale University.
All rights reserved. This book may not be
reproduced, in whole or in part, in any form
(except by reviewers for the public press),
without written permission from the publishers.
Library of Congress catalog card number: 69–15458
Designed by Helen Frisk Buzyna,
set in Times Roman type,
and printed in the United States of America by
The Carl Purington Rollins Printing-Office
of the Yale University Press.
Distributed in Great Britain, Europe, Asia, and
Africa by Yale University Press Ltd., London; in
Canada by McGill University Press, Montreal; and
in Latin America by Centro Interamericano de Libros
Académicos, Mexico City.

Preface

> The speaker has ordinarily *an attitude to his listener.* He chooses or arranges his words differently as his audience varies, in automatic or deliberate *recognition of his relation to them.* The tone of his utterance reflects his awareness of this relation, his sense of how he stands towards those he is addressing.[1]

The tone of I. A. Richards' writings on language and literature is so striking, so obtrusive, that the reader cannot help picturing the author as he reads: the brash, impatient, perhaps glib, but always clearheaded iconoclast behind such works as *Principles of Literary Criticism* (1924) and *Science and Poetry* (1926); the wise, unassuming, somewhat vague guide behind the essays in *Speculative Instruments* (1955). Without the advantage of Richards' own discussion of tone, quoted above from *Practical Criticism,* the reader might wonder whether the author underwent severe alterations in personality between writing the earlier and the later works; with it in mind, he

1. I. A. Richards, *Practical Criticism: A Study of Literary Judgment* (London, 1930; first publ. 1929), p. 182.

83826

need only assume that Richards sensed a change in his audience which demanded a different stance. In any event, tone remains perhaps the most memorable feature of Richards' writings, and the one which will ensure their continuing appeal.

Nevertheless, the obtrusiveness of his style is unfortunate, for it is partly to this that we can attribute the dearth of supporters for Richards. A good indication that his views on literature are rarely taken as seriously today as they should be is his widespread reputation as one of the founders of the New Criticism, that is, as one who has had a very important influence on that critical movement. This portrayal of Richards suggests that his work is primarily of historic interest, rather than of contemporary significance, a suggestion borne out in the historic emphasis of recent critical writing on his works. Indeed, Richards' place in the history of literary criticism, both with respect to the sources he drew upon in his writings and to his influence on later critics, has been so emphasized in the recent literature—particularly in the work of Hyman, Wimsatt and Brooks, and Wellek—that little remains to be said on the topic.[2] Any judgment concerning the popularity of a writer is bound to be largely subjective, but I should say that most students of English criticism have a rather negative view of the contemporary value of Richards' theory of literature.

This is not entirely attributable to the tone of his writings; in part it stems from the confusing fluctuation in his point of view. Nevertheless, Richards' style of writing is the first barrier which the reader encounters. The cocky confidence in "science" of his early works doubtless had a certain positive shock value. Talk of such things as "impulses," "neurology," and "psycho-

2. Stanley Edgar Hyman, *The Armed Vision* (New York, 1952), ch. 11; W. K. Wimsatt, Jr. and Cleanth Brooks, *Literary Criticism, A Short History* (New York, 1957), chs. 27 and 28; and René Wellek, "On Rereading I. A. Richards," *The Southern Review,* n.s. 3 (1967), 533–54.

logical contexts" helped put an end to windy speculations about the poet and the universe then still fashionable in criticism. But now, more than four decades later, such jolts are no longer necessary, and the belligerence of the early works, though still refreshing, serves only to distort Richards' meaning. On the other hand, the questioning indecisiveness of the later works was never very effective. To suggest many possible avenues of inquiry rather than to assert a single interpretation is an extremely effective method of teaching poetry, as shown by the widespread imitation of *Practical Criticism,* where this "protocol" approach is adopted. A questioning approach, however, when used in the development of theories concerning language and literature (a piece in *Speculative Instruments* consists entirely of questions) has never appealed to more than a few. The later works do have a special flavor, but this probably has alienated more readers than it has attracted; and, more to the point, it has again managed to obscure what Richards is trying to say.

In addition to the distorted tone of his writings, I have mentioned a second cause for Richards' current unpopularity: his confusing fluctuation in point of view. In common with many other literary theorists, Richards tends to conflate the diverse interests of different individuals concerned with literature—the aesthetician, the critic, the reader, and the moralist. Thus, even where the style is felicitous, Richards outlines a disappointingly unclear literary theory.

Despite these weaknesses of Richards' writings, I have long been convinced that he proposes in them an extremely valuable and contemporary approach to literature. The brilliance of isolated passages (such as Chapter 32 of *Principles,* "The Imagination") and the cogency of the ideas which he presented in a course at Harvard in the "Interpretation of Poetry" led me to this belief. To test it, however, I have had to extract

Richards' theory of literature from his writings by using techniques designed to minimize the distorting effects of his style and to provide a systematic structure for his observations.

Assuming that Richards' views have not changed so markedly as has his mode of presentation, I pit the clear but misleading early works against the cloudy but suggestive later ones. Thus I can remove the obscurity from the later works by seeing them as providing correctives to the ambiguities and distortions of the earlier. I also provide a systematic structure for Richards' observations by distinguishing sharply among the diverse interests of the different individuals concerned with literature, and by regrouping and analyzing Richards' writings according to these distinctions.

My techniques for exposing Richards' theory of literature have shaped the development of this study. In Chapter 1, I present what I take to be a rather widespread understanding and evaluation of Richards' writings on literature as shown by the common criticisms of them which have appeared in the literature of the last forty years. The negative picture which emerges should not be misunderstood. This familiar critical ground is an important place to start in order to develop support for the positive account of Richards' work which follows.

In Chapter 2, I introduce the framework used in the central chapters of my book to structure Richards' writings. *Coleridge on Imagination,* perhaps Richards' richest work, affords the best occasion for development of this structure because it, more than any other, suffers from confusion of the different interests of aesthetician, critic, reader, and moralist. When these interests are disentangled, *Coleridge* is seen to suggest a coherent and valuable theory of literature. This theory needs to be amplified by material from other of Richards' works, but it exists in its entirety—if only in outline—in *Coleridge.* The second reason for beginning the study of Richards' literary theory with *Coleridge* is that this work, written in 1932, marks the transition between his early, iconoclastic works, such as *Principles of Literary Criticism,* and his late, nondirectional works, such as *How To Read a Page* and *Speculative Instruments.* Discovery of the outline of a theory in this transitional work indicates the value of looking to all of Richards' works in order to fill in details and also provides justification for pitting these works against one another to minimize the distorting effects of their style.

In Chapters 3, 4, and 5, I present the three major facets of Richards' theory of literature, which deal respectively with the concerns of aesthetician, critic and reader, and moralist. The approach in each case is the same: a study of the earlier writings yields incompletely developed notions, radical ambiguities, and oversimplified models. Nonetheless, these inadequate early writings do indicate the most fruitful ways of approaching the later writings to uncover Richards' central views in each of the areas mentioned. One noteworthy result of the investigations in these three chapters is the new light shed on doctrines familiar to literary theorists. Richards likes to relate his ideas to those of previous thinkers. But, in saying that poetry is a living thing and that it is the legislator of mankind, Richards is not simply echoing his predecessors' views. (Indeed, several historians of literary criticism have found fault with the way in which he has interpreted his sources, particularly Coleridge.[3]) Rather, he cites them as labels for the convenience of his readers; his own explications of these notions, we shall discover, are truly fresh and valuable.

In Chapter 6, I show how the themes developed in the preceding three chapters may be drawn together into a coherent theory of literature. Some criticisms are raised, but, in con-

3. See e.g., D. G. James, *Scepticism and Poetry* (London, 1937), p. 8.

clusion, it is found to be sound and provocative, a far cry from the inadequate theory attributed to Richards by the average critic of Chapter 1, to whom we shall now turn.

St. Louis, Missouri
December 1967

Acknowledgments

I owe a special debt of thanks to my teacher, Monroe C. Beardsley, for first interesting me in the problems of aesthetics; to my colleagues Richard S. Rudner for encouraging me to write and Richard A. Watson for forcing me to write English; to Knox College and Washington University for helping to finance this study; to my wife, Wendy, and my daughters, Christa and Lisa, for putting up with me-and-I. A. Richards for a long time; and, not the least, to I. A. Richards himself.

Contents

I. A. Richards' Theory of Literature

1

Richards and the Average Critic: The Problem of Change and Continuity

> As to *Principles,* I regard it still with a benevolent eye as being a better sermon than it knew itself to be. . . . In general, what influence the book has had would have been different if more of those who have discussed it had read it. But every author says this![1]

Petulance such as this is rare in Richards. Usually he takes upon himself most of the blame for the misunderstandings of his writings.[2] In any event, whether he or his readers are to blame, he has been widely misinterpreted and misjudged. A sketch of the average critic's distorted understanding and judgment will provide a good beginning for a study of Richards' theory of literature, for with it we can start to see what he is really saying, and whether what he says is worthwhile.

Here, then, is the average critic's I. A. Richards:

> Richards may be important as one of the founders of the New Criticism. This can be due only to his conviction that

1. I. A. Richards, *Speculative Instruments* (Chicago, 1955), p. 44n.
2. See, e.g., I. A. Richards, *Coleridge on Imagination* (New York, 1935), p. xv; I. A. Richards, *Science and Poetry* (2nd ed. London, 1935), p. 92.

3

poetry is important and to his technique for studying it. His theory of poetry is absurd: he claims that the only way to study poetry is through psychology; he maintains that poetry does not say anything, so it has nothing to do with our beliefs. No wonder he lost interest in poetry years ago and started worrying about Basic English and general education.

Asked to expand what he takes to be Richards' claim *that the only way to study poetry is through psychology* the critic remarks that on page 116 of *Principles of Literary Criticism*[3] appears one of the most offensive *aides de penser* of modern times. Across the top of the page are printed the words "Arcadia, Night, a Cloud, Pan, and the Moon," in a straight line. Lines drawn from each of these words converge in a schematic representation of an eye, situated slightly below them in the middle of the page. Beneath the eye the lines diverge into a second line of the same words, printed in capital letters and underlined. But it is what appears below this second line of words which is truly ludicrous. Springing from the straight lines that underline the words are other, ganglionic lines, obviously meant to represent nerves, complete with endings. Interspersed in the network of "nerves" are six sorts of special symbols, a key for which is presented below the diagram. Along the edge of the diagram there is a numbered, bracketed, running commentary.

This diagram occurs in a chapter entitled "The Analysis of a Poem" and is itself intended to depict the reading of a poem. Though Richards claims that such a spatial metaphor is a danger "only to the unwary" (p. 117), the average critic contends that it epitomizes the absurd lengths to which he is pushed

3. New York, 1924.

in his discussion of poetry in *Principles*. Richards here defines a poem as a set of experiences similar to a standard experience (pp. 226–27). Experiences are happenings in the nervous system—or, rather, consist of the interactions of the energy elements of that system, the impulses (ch. 11). The experience called a poem, however, is different in two ways from other experiences: it is *communicated* to us, and it is particularly *valuable*. The experience we have on reading the words of the poem is a communicated one in that a similar experience was formerly undergone by the poet. His experience is embodied in the words of the poem in such a way that it is relived by the reader (chs. 4, 21). If our experience while reading is not essentially similar to the poet's, we can be said not to have "read" the poem at all. The value of any experience, Richards claims, is measured by the interaction of its constituent impulses. One experience is more valuable than another when it contains a harmonious interplay of more diversified impulses, when it manifests a greater unity-in-variety (ch. 7). The most valuable experiences are those in which there is such an interplay of impulses that none of them ever eventuates in overt action, but each takes its place in an equilibrium or balance. In such an experience "attitudes," or "tendencies to action," take the place of actions. Richards goes so far as to claim that a peculiar experience of this sort is a poem (chs. 8, 16).

The unsympathetic critic goes on to expand what he takes to be Richards' claim *that poetry does not say anything, so it has nothing to do with our beliefs.* In *Science and Poetry,*[4] Richards claims that "we need no beliefs, and indeed we must have none, if we are to read *King Lear*" (p. 72). A similar statement had appeared two years earlier in *Principles,* but this one epitomizes Richards' dismissal of religion as a thing of the

4. New York, 1926.

past, and its replacement by a poetry which says nothing. *Science and Poetry* is, for the most part, a summary and popularization of *Principles*. It outdoes the earlier work, however, in its sweeping claims for poetry. Poetry is said to be not merely valuable in itself but a panacea for the world's ills. Now that science (in Richards' opinion) has proven religion to be untenable, poetry alone can supply us with the moral strength needed in this unfriendly world (chs. 5–6). Strangely enough, it does so by saying nothing about this world. Statements in poetry are valuable only to the extent that they help lead to valuable balances of impulses; their incidental truth or falsity, or our belief in them, is irrelevant. Statements in poetry are thus "pseudo-statements" which call merely for acceptance and not for belief (p. 67). Active belief or disbelief in their truth or falsity results from misapprehension of their function and can lead only to misreading. It is for this reason that Richards claims we need believe nothing (and should believe nothing) in order to read *King Lear:* if we do let our beliefs interfere with our reading, we will undoubtedly miss everything that is valuable in the experience.

The critic cites related themes, regarding "pseudo-statement" merely as a new name for the "emotive language" of *The Meaning of Meaning*.[5] In the earlier book, Richards draws a distinction between the emotive and symbolic uses of language: language is used emotively to express or excite feelings and attitudes; symbolically, it is used to record or communicate thoughts concerning features of the external world (pp. 257–58). The language of science is symbolic; the language of poetry emotive (pp. 372–78). The language of religion fails both

5. C. K. Ogden and I. A. Richards, *The Meaning of Meaning, A Study of the Influence of Language upon Thought and of the Science of Symbolism* (New York, 1926; first publ. 1923).

symbolically (the things to which it refers simply are not there) and emotively (it does not do the job poetry does in sustaining valuable states of affairs).[6]

Concerning Richards' conviction *that poetry is important and . . . his technique for studying it,* the average critic elaborates as follows. Richards viewed his third important book, *Practical Criticism,*[7] as a "companion volume" to *Principles.* Here is his comment on the substance of the book, written two years before its publication:

> Extremely good and extremely bad poems were put *unsigned* before a large and able audience. The comments they wrote at leisure give, as it were, a stereoscopic view of the poem and of possible opinion on it. This material when systematically analysed, provides, not only an interesting commentary upon the state of contemporary culture, but a new and powerful educational instrument.[8]

The results of the experiment were, and continue to be, unsettling. Without the crutch of knowing the poets, students studying for an Honours degree in English at Cambridge University proved to be remarkably imperceptive. (And few readers who have read the book and played the game fairly—that is, without first looking up the authors in the appendix—have managed much better.) A few of Richards' critics were incredulous, suspecting either his method or the general intelligence of the students.[9] But the typical reaction, well captured

---

6. *Science and Poetry,* chs. 5–6.

7. London, 1930; first publ. 1929.

8. *Principles of Literary Criticism* (3rd ed. New York, 1955; first publ. 1928), p. 4.

9. See, e.g., Edward Shanks, "An Experiment with Literature," *Saturday Review, 147* (1929), 865–66.

in a review which opens with the description of a nightmare inspired by the book, was one of dismay mixed with horror.[10]

In *Practical Criticism,* Richards classified the mistakes made by his readers into ten typical errors, including such now familiar snares as sentimentality, stock responses, doctrinal adhesion, and technical presuppositions (pp. 13–17; pt. 3). He sketched several programs for improving the situation: the study of language as such, a careful consideration of aims in the teaching of English, and an increased awareness on the reader's part of the pitfalls in reading (pt. 4). The great value of *Practical Criticism* does not lie in Richards' programs, however, but in his classification and discussion of typical mistakes in reading; in his conviction that poems are worth consideration in their own right, independent of their authors; and in the tremendously effective technique for teaching poetry.

With regard to his claim that Richards *lost interest in poetry years ago and started worrying about Basic English and general education,* the average critic notes that, although it was during the Second World War that Richards worked hard to promote a new world language, his interest in Basic English actually began in the early 1930's, with the development of the language by his friend and collaborator, C. K. Ogden. Though he claims otherwise, Richards' involvement with this barbaric invention clearly shows a growing lack of interest in poetry. Basic English has a vocabulary of 850 words; it eschews complexity and richness. Yet during the war Richards not only repeatedly spoke highly of the language, but even wrote several books in it, including translations of Homer's *Iliad* and Plato's *Republic.* (Concerning the latter, one critic justly remarked

10. E. G. Twitchett, "A Vision of Judgment," *London Mercury, 20* (1929), 598–605. See also L. Woolf, "How Not to Read Poetry," *Nation and Athenaeum, 45* (1929), 538.

that Plato did not write in Basic Greek.)[11] Since the war he has used Basic English to develop a pictorial method for teaching foreign languages and has concerned himself with other problems in education.

It must by now be apparent that the average critic's view of Richards' work is neither well integrated nor carefully worked out. Yet the impression is surprisingly widespread: Richards reduces poems to impulses; he thinks that poetry will save us but cannot tell us how, for he claims that it has nothing to do with the world; he has shown us an excellent way to teach poetry, but he is no longer much concerned with poetry; he is occupied instead with the lowest common denominator—basic language and unspecialized learning. Pressed to elaborate his obvious dissatisfaction with Richards' views, the critic might well say:

> *The distinction between the emotive and the referential uses of language is much too sharp. His general theory of value is unconvincing; his picture of the value of poetry laughable. The reduction of poetry to impulses spells the end of poetry.*

To fill out his statement that *the distinction between the emotive and the referential uses of language is much too sharp,* the critic would comment on two major problems. First, the rift between the two uses shows that Richards feels that emotions and attitudes aroused in the course of the poetic experience are not directed toward specific aspects of the individual's

11. Eric Russell Bentley, "The Early I. A. Richards," *Rocky Mountain Review, 8* (1944), 36.

environment. But poetry is not concerned with emotions and attitudes in isolation. It is not enough for references to arouse feelings; they must also refer to the things to which these feelings are directed.[12] Second, Richards' distinction does not provide an adequate place for considerations of truth and belief in poetry. He excludes such considerations because he feels that judging a poem from the standpoint of its truth or falsity is a misuse of the poem and always leads to misevaluation. Nevertheless, truth can sometimes enhance poetic statements, even though it is not the function of such statements to express the truth.[13] Belief may supply the framework in which the poem must be read to be properly appreciated. No one who does not believe that Cordelia is good and that Edmund is evil can truly grasp *King Lear*. Such beliefs cannot be merely accepted; they must really be held.[14]

12. See, e.g., Thomas C. Pollock, "A Critique of I. A. Richards' Theory of Language and Literature," *A Theory of Meaning Analyzed,* Monograph III, General Semantics Monographs, ed. M. Kending (Chicago, 1942), p. 10; John Crowe Ransom, *The New Criticism* (Norfolk, 1942), pp. 20–22, 28, 35; Max Black, "Some Questions about Emotive Meaning," A Symposium on Emotive Meaning, *Philosophical Review, 57* (1948), 115–17; William Empson, *The Structure of Complex Words* (London, 1952), pp. 6–7.

13. See, e.g., T. S. Eliot, "Religion and Literature," *Selected Essays* (new ed. New York, 1950), pp. 343–54; Frederick A. Pottle, *The Idiom of Poetry* (Ithaca, 1946), pp. 191–96; W. K. Wimsatt, Jr., "Poetry and Morals, A Relation Reargued," *The Verbal Icon* (University of Kentucky, 1954), pp. 85–100, esp. pp. 96–99; Alexander Sesonske, "Truth in Art," *Journal of Philosophy, 53* (1956), 345–53; Manuel Bilsky, "I. A. Richards on Belief," *Philosophy and Phenomenological Research, 12* (1951), 114–15.

14. See, e.g., Jerome Stolnitz, *Aesthetics and the Philosophy of Art Criticism* (Boston, 1960), pp. 331–32; M. H. Abrams, "Belief and the Suspension of Disbelief," *English Institute Essays,* 1957 (New York, 1958), pp. 1–30, esp. pp. 16–21.

Other difficulties result from the split between emotive and referential uses of language. Richards' view of science is overly Victorian, and the completely neutral world which he pictures, a mechanical world with neither mystery nor place for wonder, is not the scientific world of the twentieth century.[15] His stand on religion is confusing and unsatisfactory: religion today is not vying with science and certainly cannot be replaced by poetry; it fulfills needs different from those fulfilled by either of these disciplines.[16]

The average critic continues in order to expand his claim that Richards' *general theory of value is unconvincing and that his picture of the value of poetry is laughable*. Richards' belief that the value of an experience is determined by a balance of impulses is overly subjective. Experiences which reflect the satisfaction of a greater number of diverse impulses may be preferred by some individuals, but this is no reason for calling them better than experiences which reflect narrower satisfactions.[17] His extrapolation of this preferential theory to the social sphere is uncritical, for he does not take into account the social context of all individual choices.[18] The theory is vague: is value determined quantitatively or qualitatively? And it is mysterious: conscious facets of the valuable experience are cor-

15. See, e.g., Bentley, *Rocky Mountain Review, 8,* 35; Alick West, *Crisis and Criticism* (London, 1937), pp. 70–71.

16. See, e.g., T. S. Eliot, "Literature, Science and Dogma," *Dial, 82* (1927), 237–43; G. Rostrevor Hamilton, *Poetry and Contemplation* (Cambridge, 1937), pp. 150 ff.

17. See, e.g., S. L. Bethell, "Suggestions toward a Theory of Value," *Criterion, 14* (1935), 241–42; D. W. Harding, "I. A. Richards," *Scrutiny, 1* (1933), 329; E. H. Knight, "Some Aesthetic Theories of Mr. Richards," *Mind, 36* (1927), 74; Eliseo Vivas, "Four Notes on I. A. Richards' Aesthetic Theory," *Philosophical Review, 44* (1935), 367.

18. Bethell, *Criterion, 14,* 241; David Daiches, "The Principles of Literary Criticism," *New Republic, 98* (1939), 97–98.

11

SALEM COLLEGE LIBRARY
WINSTON-SALEM, N. C.

rected by unobservable "impulses."[19] Richards' claim that a poem is valuable in the same way that any other experience is valuable—for the poem and other experiences are qualitatively similar—is clearly false: we might as well say that the experience of looking at a painting is qualitatively similar to those undergone on the way to the gallery. A poem affords a unique experience.[20]

Richards deserves the ridicule of his critics for his exaggeration of the instrumental value of poetry: "Poetry 'is capable of saving us,' he says; it is like saying that the wall-paper will save us when the walls have crumbled."[21] Richards certainly has not proven that poetry can save a civilization; he has merely *said* that it can.

Finally, the average critic supports his claim that Richards' *reduction of poetry to impulses spells the end of poetry* by pointing out that, since Richards' "psychology" is not real psychology, his reduction does not clarify anything. He has observed none of the canons of scientific method in his own attempt to replace the obscurities of previous theories. His "impulses" are not themselves available for inspection, nor do they function as unobservable theoretical entities, such as atoms. Indeed, they seem to be little more than pseudo-quali-

19. See, e.g., C. P. Aiken, "A Scientific Approach to Criticism," *Nation and Athenaeum, 36* (1925), 586; Black, *Philosophical Review, 57,* 118; Hamilton, *Poetry and Contemplation,* ch. 2; Harding, *Scrutiny, 1,* 331; Bentley, *Rocky Mountain Review, 8,* 29.

20. See, e.g., Hamilton, *Poetry and Contemplation,* pp. 89–95, chs. 9–12; D. G. James, *Scepticism and Poetry* (London, 1937), pp. 75, 130–34; Roger Fry, *Transformations* (Garden City, 1956), pp. 2–13; Max Eastman, *The Literary Mind* (New York, 1932), pp. 311–12; Montgomery Belgion, "What Is Criticism?" *Criterion, 10* (1930), 126; Knight, *Mind, 36,* 75–76.

21. Eliot, *Dial, 82,* 243. See also Eastman, *Literary Mind,* pp. 313–17; Vivas, *Philosophical Review, 44,* 357–58.

ties.[22] As such, they may be harmless enough, but one result of
the purported reduction is more serious. Richards' talk about
impulses has led him to replace the poem with the *results* of the
poem, to commit the affective fallacy. Given such a reduction,
one might as well substitute a judicious dose of a harmless drug
for the poem; it conceivably could have the same results.[23]

The average critic is an intelligent and serious one. He is not
the sort of scholar who thinks that Richards' work is an elaborate attack on poetry in favor of science simply because
Richards calls the statements of poetry *"pseudo-*statements,"
which, of course, means that they must all be false.[24] Nevertheless, he may very well be misinterpreting Richards because he is
not familiar with the whole range of Richards' writings. He has
read *Principles of Literary Criticism, Practical Criticism,* and
Science and Poetry and has probably skimmed *The Meaning
of Meaning, Coleridge on Imagination,* and *How To Read a*

22. See, e.g., Harding, *Scrutiny, 1,* 331–33; Hamilton, *Poetry and
Contemplation,* ch. 3; Black, *Philosophical Review, 57,* 117–18; Ransom, *New Criticism,* pp. 12–13; Allen Tate, *On the Limits of Poetry*
(New York, 1948), pp. 42–43; Max Black, "Some Objections to Ogden
and Richards' Theory of Interpretation," *Journal of Philosophy, 39*
(1942), 286–88; Bentley, *Rocky Mountain Review, 8,* 31.

23. See, e.g., Ransom, *New Criticism,* pp. 31–32; James, *Scepticism
and Poetry,* p. 57; W. K. Wimsatt, Jr., "The Affective Fallacy," *Verbal
Icon,* pp. 21–39, esp. 28–29; Vivas, *Philosophical Review, 44,* 360–62;
H. M. McLuhan, "Poetic vs. Rhetorical Exegesis," *Sewanee Review, 52*
(1944), 268; Murray Krieger, *The New Apologists for Poetry* (Minneapolis, 1956), pp. 115–17; Knight, *Mind, 36,* 72. Compare Gerald
Allen Rudolph, *The Affective Criticism of I. A. Richards.* Unpubl. Ph.D.
dissert., University of Washington, 1959.

24. See Tate, *On the Limits of Poetry,* pp. 9–11, also p. 108. See also
James, *Scepticism and Poetry,* pp. 68–70; Pollock, *Theory of Meaning
Analyzed,* pp. 12, 19.

13

Page. But it is unlikely that he knows *The Philosophy of Rhetoric* or *Interpretation in Teaching,* and it is almost certain that he is unfamiliar with *Speculative Instruments* or the many short pieces which have appeared in periodicals over the past thirty years.

This is not surprising. Difficult as the classification of these last works may be (I understand that the question of how to classify *Speculative Instruments* is used in advanced tests in library schools), there is little here to entice the critic. If Richards' own hints of a change in his interests are considered along with the seeming irrelevance of these works to literary theory, their neglect is assured.[25] But this is doubly unfortunate: not only are some of Richards' most illuminating statements on poetry, such as the essay "Poetry as an Instrument of Research," hidden in these less-known works, but many discussions, such as the analyses of translation procedures and philosophy, which apparently have little to do with literary matters clarify puzzles arising in his theory of literature. It is obvious that the relevance of such analyses can be established only by using the later writings to develop Richards' literary theory. This I shall do in the following chapters. Here I want merely to suggest a possible source of the average critic's misinterpretations, and the obvious corrective.

Even if the critic became convinced of the relevance of the later writings, however, it is not assured that he would agree that the statements and judgments attributed to him above are distortions. He might argue that this picture of Richards is the early Richards; Richards' later writings are material for a late Richards. And, he might add, the late Richards is a changed

25. See *The Philosophy of Rhetoric,* The Mary Flexner Lectures on the Humanities, III (New York, 1936), p. 49; *Speculative Instruments,* p. 93; "The Future of Poetry," *The Screens and Other Poems* (New York, 1960), p. 127.

and chastened man. Perhaps Richards needed to accept "positivism" so that he could reject it so effectively.[26] In any event, the average critic might claim that there are two theories of literature in Richards' writings.[27]

There is some evidence for such a change in Richards' thought. Anyone acquainted with *The Meaning of Meaning* or *Science and Poetry* would think that *Speculative Instruments* had been written by a different author. The brash, cocksure tone of the earlier works has given way to a hesitant and timid one; assertions have been replaced by questions. Moreover, the change is not merely one of tone. Obvious demons of the early works, including Plato, have become idols of the later works.[28] Richards even seems to have supplied a transitional work, *Coleridge on Imagination*, in which he investigates the work of the extreme idealist from the standpoint of a materialist.[29]

The plausibilty of any radical change is lessened, however, by Richards' own comments on the development of his writings. The original preface to *Coleridge* ends with this statement: "So far as I am able to judge, I am not in these interpretations departing from the general positions assumed in my earlier books. I find them, when allowance has been made for changes in vo-

26. See R. P. Blackmur, "San Giovanni in Venere: Allen Tate as a Man of Letters," *Sewanee Review, 67* (1959), 621.

27. See, e.g., Black, *Philosophical Review, 57,* 120; Ransom, *New Criticism,* pp. 74–75; Empson, *Structure of Complex Words,* p. 14; Tate, *On the Limits of Poetry, pp.* 41–45. Compare Gerald E. Graff, "The Later Richards and the New Criticism," in *Criticism, 9* (1967), 229–42.

28. Compare *Meaning of Meaning,* pp. 45–47 with I. A. Richards, *How To Read a Page, A Course in Efficient Reading with an Introduction to a Hundred Great Words* (New York, 1942), chs. 11–12.

29. *Coleridge,* p. 19.

cabulary, the same, though, I hope, developed" (p. xv). In a late essay he remarks: "In rereading *Principles* . . . , I am more impressed by its anticipations of my later views than by the occurrence of anything to retract. I changed my vocabulary and my metaphors somewhat . . . to present much the same views again."[30] Richards may, of course, be unaware of important changes in his thought, or be radically misinterpreting his own earlier writings. But close comparison of the earlier and later works makes this seem unlikely.

I find both change and continuity in Richards' work. While I would agree with Richards that there has been a change in his mode of presenting similar ideas, I would add that the modes of presentation adopted in the earlier and later works have had crucial effects of their own. His use of the impulse theory to present his ideas in the early works had the effect of forcing him to certain conclusions not in keeping with the general trend of his thought; this accounts, in large part, for the inconsistencies and ambiguities of the early writings. On the other hand, the fluctuating, free, almost poetic style of the later works has hidden many of his most important points from his readers. I agree that *Coleridge on Imagination* is a transitional work—not, however, one in which his ideas change, but one in which he is forsaking the misleading framework of the earlier books and adopting the obscure style of the later.

The peculiarities of Richards' writings determine the approach needed to uncover his theory of literature. It is easy, but fruitless, to criticize Richards for his oversimplified scientism or for his obscurity. One must, instead, use the inconsistencies and ambiguities implicit in the scientistic scheme to indicate the proper interpretation of the difficult later writings. This is the approach I have adopted in later chapters of this book. But

30. *Speculative Instruments,* p. 53n.

before embarking on an investigation of the whole of Richards' work, I shall take a close look at the largely neglected *Coleridge on Imagination,* a book which not only presents all the difficulties one might expect from such a transitional work but which also offers tantalizing hints of Richards' whole complex theory of literature.

2

Coleridge on Imagination: *A Summary and an Analysis*

To put the burden of constituting an order for our minds on the poet may seem unfair. It is not the philosopher, however, or the moralist who puts it on him, but birth.[1]

Coleridge on Imagination is a difficult book to take seriously. Richards' exaggerations are at first amusing: as a critic, Coleridge offers "glimpses of a new possible theoretic order—behind them hope for new power thence; behind that again a regress of visions, of the rectified mind and the freed heart" (p. xiv). Coleridge's theory of poetry replaces metaphysics and morals by showing their problems to be "artificial" and their methods "inadequate" (p. 20). When "Coleridge's grounds for the distinction" between imagination and fancy and his "applications of it" have "entered our general intellectual tradition," "the order of our universes will have been changed" (p. 72). "It is the privilege of poetry to preserve us from mistaking our notions either for things or for ourselves" (p. 163). The best poetry establishes the "norms of value" (p. 214). Amusement is

1. *Coleridge,* p. 227.

18

replaced by irritation, however, when the aesthetician is unable to discover any clear support for these claims in Richards' argument. The grandiose pronouncements loom up unpredictably from the swirl of ramblings in idealistic metaphysics, digressions on the use of theory, and excursions into Coleridgean criticism.

The critic may appreciate these excursions, but practically everything else will exasperate him. "One wonders," F. R. Leavis muses, "in what state the matter of [the more abstruse and ambitious chapters] . . . in the original discussions and lectures, must have left literary students. . . ."[2] To this puzzlement we must add annoyance at Richards' frequent quotation of scattered poetic lines without comment, and resentment at his blanket, unjustified dismissal of contemporary criticism.

In a characteristically violent review of the work, Leavis underscores these weaknesses. Despite pretensions of ignorance of the philosophic material, he gains the support of the aesthetician by exposing Richards' equivocations on theoretical points. He emphasizes the vagueness and incompleteness of Richards' critical comments in his detailed discussions of Richards' references to particular poets and poetry. The reader, whether aesthetician or critic, finds difficulty in disagreeing with Leavis' effective dismissal of the book: "That [Richards'] literary interests derive from an interest in theory rather than his theory from his literary interests has never been a secret."[3]

One cannot rescue Richards' work by pointing out that most of Leavis' countersuggestions are based only on assertion or appeals to the *cognoscenti*. Instead, one must show that the work really illuminates the nature of literature. In order to

---

2. F. R. Leavis, "Dr. Richards, Bentham and Coleridge," *Scrutiny, 3* (1935), 385.
3. Ibid., p. 400.

accomplish that task, I shall summarize *Coleridge* and then suggest a way of unscrambling Richards' confusing presentation. The summary occupies the first section of this chapter, while in the second section I develop a way of approaching the book which yields hints of Richards' highly significant theory of literature.

The following chapter-by-chapter summary of *Coleridge* avoids interpretation of Richards' views except on a few points. The argument is basically Richards'. The summary is by no means exhaustive, however. In particular, I have avoided Richards' discussions of the problems facing the interpreter of Coleridge's writings. Since my aim is to arrive at an accurate understanding of Richards' understanding, the very difficult task of evaluating his interpretation as such need not be attempted.

Preface

Here, Richards' strikes several themes which he expands later in the book. He will treat Coleridge as a "semasiologist," a person who realized that a study of the meanings of words illuminates all life activities. This study, with particular attention to poetry, should transform criticism, with its present goals of social communion, into a more serious endeavor. Richards cautions that his interpretations of Coleridge may be wrong, but adds that if they encourage interest in the topic, they will have accomplished their purpose.

Chapter I: The First Range of Hills

The focus of "The First Range of Hills" is a passage from Coleridge's *Biographia Literaria* allegorizing the limitations of men's understanding and aspirations. Most men are content to live in the valley of life, without questioning their own natures or the nature of their environment. A few, however, spend their lives on the first range of hills, trying to discern the sources of life. One of these persons was Coleridge. His true value as a critic comes from his philosophic speculations, although as a philosopher he was actually a failure. However, if we take his philosophy as a symbol of his "psychology," his views concerning the nature of the mind and its relation to its environment, we find insights that undercut much current philosophy. Richards sketches an important shift in Coleridge's thought concerning the nature of the mind during the period 1800–01, when he gave up an associationistic, Hartleian theory for an organic, Kantian theory. Coleridge did not actually abandon his earlier theory, but incorporated it into his later one. Or, to be more precise, he held to it as a way of surveying the mind. Richards expands this last point to explain why he thinks that the study of Coleridge's views is so worthwhile. By treating them as instruments, as machinery, as systems to be thought *with,* not *about*—and Richards claims that this was often characteristic of Coleridge's own approach toward his doctrines—we come to understand ourselves. This constitutes a utilitarian justification for the study of idealism. The insight, the "realizing act of intuition," by which much current philosophy is shown to be superceded, comes through this instrumental use of doctrines.

Chapter II: Adumbrations

We need not concern ourselves in detail with "Adumbrations." Here Richards distinguishes the theory of imagination which he will develop from some other doctrines with which it might be, or has been, confused. He sometimes hints at the doctrine to come, for instance in his discussion of Muratori's conception of the poet's imagination, which unites and enlivens simple ideas. But most of the chapter is devoted to a criticism of modern theorists, such as Lowes and Abercrombie, whose claim that the distinction between imagination and fancy is merely one of degree clearly disregards Coleridge's explicit cautions on this matter. Coleridge, a psychologist, knew the dangers of attributing different psychological phenomena to differences in degree.

Chapter III: The Coalescence of Subject and Object

In "The Coalescence of Subject and Object," Richards introduces many of the technical terms which Coleridge used to develop his Schellingean conception of the mind. "Coalescence of subject and object" explains the working of the "imagination." To understand this coalescence we must use "philosophy," whose method is the "inner sense." This inner sense is developed to different degrees in different individuals. Those with the most highly developed inner sense are aware of their own acts of comprehending. Such awareness Coleridge calls the "realizing intuition," which produces the "first postulate of philosophy . . . Know thyself." In this highest operation of the inner sense, we have the prime example of the coalescence of subject and object, for in knowing itself, the mind makes itself. Realizing intuition is distinguished from simple introspection, where there is no creation in the course of discovery. Here, in contrast, nothing is discovered which is not created; the self is freely made as it is discovered. For endeavors in which theory and practice must be separated, we need to distinguish the knowing subject from the object known. But in the realizing intuition, we can no more distinguish knowledge from what is known than we can distinguish, in a plant, "growledge" from what is grown. Richards acknowledges that the view that subject and object coalesce in the realizing intuition is a puzzling one, in contrast to the more commonsensical separation embodied in the model supplied by physical science. It is a view which must be adhered to in practice to be grasped.

Coleridge used the notion of coalescence to introduce his account of the imagination. According to him, there are two sorts of imagination, the primary and the secondary. The primary imagination, the "repetition in the finite mind of the eternal act of creation," produces the perceptual world of the senses. The secondary imagination, the echo of the primary, infuses this world with poetry and "every aspect of the routine world in which it is invested with other values than these necessary for our bare continuance as living beings" (p. 58). Thus there is a common source for poetry and the other values of civilized life, and hence a relation between them. Both sorts of imagination are vital, in contrast to the mechanical power of fancy, which merely collects and rearranges the units previously produced by the creative, growing power of imagination.

Richards reviews some of the puzzles that Coleridge encountered in developing the implications of this account for freedom and external existence, but suggests that the primary use of the hurriedly developed doctrine is not as metaphysics, but as psychology—that is, as a description of the operation of the mind. The idealist's picture of the mind as a growing activity is far superior to the associationist's picture of the mind as a set of discriminable thoughts. The former is especially suited to exploring the "most intricate and unified modes of mental activity—those in poetry" (p. 69). As Richards shows in his following chapter, however, it is possible to amalgamate the two opposed doctrines to illuminate the nature of poetry.

23

Chapter IV: Imagination and Fancy

After a few preliminaries, Richards turns, in "Imagination and Fancy," to an examination of the nature of poetic language. Every utterance, every string of words, has its own unity of meaning; its individual parts produce a joint effect. Richards contrasts the relation of these parts by the "coadunating imagination," or "esemplastic power" ("bringing into one power"), and the "fancy," or "aggregating power," in this way:

> In Imagination the parts of the meaning—both as regards the ways in which they are apprehended and the modes of combination of their effects in the mind—mutually modify one another.
>
> In Fancy, the parts of the meaning are apprehended as though independent of their fellow-members (as they would be if they belonged to quite other wholes) and although, of course, the parts together have a joint effect which is not what it would be if the assemblage were different, the effects of the parts remain for an interval separate and collide or combine *later,* insofar as they do so at all. (pp. 86–87)

This formal contrast is presented as an hypothesis intended to account for Coleridge's discussions of the differences between fanciful and imaginative passages from Shakespeare's *Venus and Adonis*. Richards' elaboration of the distinction suggests that the difference between imaginative and fanciful poetry is the difference between a fixed and a changing pattern of interpretation. In fancy, the interpretation given to a unit (which may be a word, a phrase, or, in Coleridge's terms, an image) to render that unit meaningful in the context in which it appears, is the same one the unit carries throughout the interpretive process. Thus, in Coleridge's example of a fanciful passage:

> Full gently now she takes him by the hand,
> A lily prison'd in a gaol of snow,
>> *(Venus and Adonis,* lines 361–62)

it is necessary to view both Venus' hand and the gaol of snow as white enclosures to understand their role in the passage. But these characteristics—together with any additional characteristics we might have initially attributed to them (Venus' hand, perhaps, as delicate and warm; the gaol of snow, perhaps, as cold and barred)—will remain the characteristics of the hand and the gaol so long as we attend to the passage. In imagination, on the contrary, the unit becomes freighted with additional meanings as interpretations are afforded other units. Thus, using Coleridge's example of an imaginative passage:

> Look! how a bright star shooteth from the sky,
> So glides he in the night from Venus' eye.
>> *(Venus and Adonis,* lines 815–16)

whereas "star" may originally have been interpreted as a "light-giver" to make sense in its context of comparison, it gains the additional meaning, "influence," in the course of our reading because of the interpretation afforded other units. Speaking of two imaginative passages, Richards remarks: "In neither passage is there a phrase which does not carry, at first unnoticed, secondary and tertiary co-implications among their possibilities of interpretation" (p. 94).

There is thus a twofold "bringing into one" accomplished by the coadunating imagination. First, the units of the poem

25

are brought into one in the sense that the growth of response in imaginative poetry requires a constant reassociation of the units of the poem with one another, rather than the single association characteristic of fancy. Second, the interpretations of each unit are brought into one in the sense that each of them contributes to the final meaning of the utterance.

Despite the positive overtones of the "growth" and "self-realization" characterizing the imaginative experience, and the "recession, roominess and richness" (p. 94) of its meaning, Richards indicates that the distinction between fanciful and imaginative experiences is not necessarily normative. Though some works are primarily imaginative or fanciful, frequently the modes of meaning are mixed, and there is a sense in which they demand one another.

Chapter IV ends with a brief discussion of ways in which we can identify the nature of a poetic passage. We can find a difference between imaginative and fanciful poetry if we "take account of . . . [the] place and function [of the imaginative or fanciful events] in the whole activity of the mind—and of this not only as an individual life but as a representative of what . . . [Coleridge] calls the *'all in each* of human nature' " (p. 97). But

> fortunately we have a more direct and surer method of identifying the work of the Imagination: namely, through the Imagination itself. . . . There is a persistent tradition . . . which recognizes acts of Imagination. Literally they are *re-cognized:* the *all in each* finds again in them the same enlargement." (pp. 97–98)

The freedom which the individual shares with all men is the ground of the immediate, intuitive feeling which is his only certain sign that he is receiving what is truly in a passage— that he is understanding the poet.

Chapter V: The Sense of Musical Delight

"The Sense of Musical Delight" of poetry is explained with the aid of the projective imagination, which must be distinguished from the coadunative imagination described in Chapter IV. There are, Richards claims, several different attitudes, ranging from nonprojective to projective, which we can adopt toward certain entities. Take, for instance, a word. A word can be viewed (1) as a set of marks on paper; (2) as such a set of marks invested with sound and movement and further qualities such as rapidity and weight which accrue from "past experience with similar speech-acts" (p. 106); and (3) as a sign containing within itself "a part or whole of the meaning" (p. 106). A word which is invested with all its meaning through the activity of the "projective imagination" is a word viewed completely projectively. Richards points to the parallel case of a poem. "How often, when we discuss a poem, do we *not* include a meaning as well as the marks on the paper, in our acting definition? A meaning is always what we are talking about, never the signs" (p. 107).

Richards uses Coleridge's conception of the projective imagination to correct Coleridge's own suggestion that the source of the musical delight of poetry lies simply in the pleasures provided by the sound of the verse. When we view the words of a poem as being invested with their meanings, meter becomes a movement of *meanings,* not simply of sounds. It is this movement in which we delight. Using Coleridgean hints, Richards thus assimilates the musical appeal of verse to the growth in meaning characteristic of the coadunative imagination. Richards incidentally notes some further features of projection. Different sorts of poetry can be distinguished by the degree to which we project meanings into their words; different critical doctrines emerge from the emphasis or de-emphasis of projection.

Chapter VI: Good Sense

Richards here explicates Coleridge's "good sense." Good sense is used by the poet to write well and by the reader to determine the nature and worth of a poem. Richards demurs at Coleridge's interpretation of good sense as conscious or unconscious "principles of grammar, logic, or psychology." Formulable theory can help us avoid misjudgments, but

> *there* its practical service ends. What should guide our decisions is something larger, . . . our experience of life and literature . . . as it is available in a power of choice. . . . It will be the modes and capacities of distinguishing that have been developed in these past reflections, rather than the *conclusions* we came to, that become the source and sanction of the choice. (p. 128)

Good sense is the technique which will help us "to recognize what we see with . . . [a speculative instrument such as the imagination] and to make sure that we are looking at what we think we are looking at . . ." (pp. 129–30). After an appraisal of Coleridge's over-literal criticism of Wordsworth's *Ode,* which he carried out under the banner of good sense, Richards concludes the chapter with a discussion of the relationship between literary theory and judgment. Judgment, whether of a passage of poetry or of a politician, depends in the final analysis upon the reason, the whole man, the combination of practical and speculative intellect. Such judgment, nonetheless, relies upon the discriminating power of theory.

Chapter VII: The Wind Harp

Two metaphysical doctrines, a "realist" and a "projective" doctrine, can be found in Wordsworth's and Coleridge's poetry.

"In the first doctrine man, through Nature, is linked with something other than himself which he perceives through her. In the second, he makes of her, as with a mirror, a transformed image of his own being" (p. 145). Though Richards devotes some time in this chapter to the way in which each poet develops the doctrines in his works through use of the wind harp image, he is more concerned to show how the two doctrines are not really in conflict with one another, at least if one reduces them to a "fact of mind which is their ground and origin" (p. 147). To concern oneself with a fact of mind is to attend not only to "what is being said" by an utterance, but also to "the saying of it." Thus, a fact of mind includes

> "what is being said," it *is* a representation of a supposed state of affairs— . . . but it includes also much more. And it represents (in a slightly different sense . . .) much more —the history of the speaker's mind, and his feelings and attitudes in the moment of speaking, and conditions of their governance in the future. (p. 143)

Richards notes four senses in which the word "nature" may be used. When we distinguish these senses, we see how the two doctrines are not contradictory when reduced to a fact of mind. "Nature-I" is "the influences . . . to which the mind is subject . . . "; "Nature-II" is the picture of the universe we project in response to I; "Nature-III" is a selection of II "which . . . [is] perceived by all men alike, . . . the world of our practical every-day experience"; "Nature-IV" is a selection from III required by physicists to give an account of I (pp. 157–58). The contrast between Nature-II and Nature-III is the same as that drawn by Richards in Chapter III between the product of the primary imagination—the "inanimate cold world," the "world of motor-buses, beef-steaks, and acquaintances" (p. 58)

—and the product of the secondary imagination—the civilized world, the world of values, the world "invested with characters derived from our own feelings, our hopes and fears, desires, and thoughts" (pp. 159–60). Richards does not make explicit how the distinction of the four senses of "nature" obviates the seeming opposition between the two metaphysical doctrines. We might interpret him in this way: for the individual to deal adequately with influences from without, he must view nature as symbolic of a further reality. (In this respect, the account represents a "state of affairs.") But this symbolization succeeds only because it is the result of a projection of his needs and desires into a story of his own creation. (Here, the account represents "in a slightly different sense . . . the history of the speaker's mind.") Richards never offers an account such as this, however, since, as doctrine, it falsifies the solution. "It is better to say . . . that our concern is with the fact of mind itself, the immediate self-consciousness in the imaginative moment which is the source of the doctrines" (p. 162). The "coalescence" of the two doctrines can be known only through the fact of mind (which Richards here likens to "poetry") and not through "abstract language."

Chapter VIII: The Boundaries of the Mythical

All of our conceptions of nature, except Nature-I, are the results of our projections, the nature of the physicist and of ordinary experience no less than that of value. This appears to be the key to the solution of the conflict between science and value which Richards pictures in "The Boundaries of the Mythical." He says:

> In the conduct of our lives we sometimes need perceptions into which our hopes and fears and desires enter as little

as possible. These are the perceptions sought by the man of science. . . . [But] wisdom requires a different co-ordination of our perceptions, yielding another Nature for us to live in—a Nature in which our hopes and fears and desires, by projection, can come to terms with one another. (pp. 169–70)

Only a return to the "self-realizing intuition" can solve this conflict. For in the imaginative moment we are at the boundary of the mythical, which includes all meanings. A "return to the fact of mind, and growth in it, is the only 'solution' of the metaphysical problem . . ." (p. 182). Richards reverts to this point at the conclusion of Chapter IX, there relating it more specifically to poetry: our different pictures of nature are all of our own making. "The sage may teach a doctrine without words; but, if so, it is a doctrine about another world than ours and for another life" (p. 230). Our worlds are radically linguistic. Of all linguistic forms, that in which there is the fullest coadunation of the parts is that in which there is the subtlest working out of our innermost needs. When words are viewed as being alive, as parts of a plant, when they are most free to interrelate with one another, they will most fully correlate, co-ordinate, and thus solve the needs from which they spring. Thus poetry, as the paradigm of such free linguistic forms, affords a measuring rod for all other myths. As the "completest mode of utterance," (p. 163) as the "myth-making which most brings 'the whole soul of man into activity' " (p. 228), it represents man's chief "co-ordinating instrument" (p. 230). And the study of the ways in which poetry *means,* becomes the most important study of all—the study which gives us "new powers over our minds comparable to those which systematic physical inquiries are giving us over our environment" (p. 232).

Richards thus sees poetry as being of particular value because it represents the return to the fact of mind which will unite fact and value. Nevertheless, poetry also appears as one of the disputants in that conflict. We saw in Richards' discussion of the secondary imagination that poetry, along with value, is a denizen of Nature-II. As such, it must be distinguished from features of the ordinary and scientific worlds of Nature-III and Nature-IV. Thus science has an absolute hold upon our actions. But our response to poetry must be limited by what we have contributed to it. To quote a familiar Coleridgean line, in poetry, "We receive but what we give" (p. 175).

Chapter IX: The Bridle of Pegasus

Most of this final chapter is devoted to a discussion of themes familiar to the aesthetician and critic. Richards here attributes the inadequacy of current criticism to the disappearance of an intellectual tradition. He pleads for a theory which will enable us to regain the skill in reading evinced in other ages. He attributes much misreading to our mistaken notions about "meaning" in poetry. There may be an abstractable prose sense in a poem (though many poems may have no such discriminable feature), but isolating this sense never gives us the poem. We must discover how the sense works in connection with other elements of the poem. Is it, for instance, a source, a tributary, or a dike?

> With the best poetry there is nowhere to arrive, no final solution. The poem is no ticket to the Fortunate Isles, or even to Purgatory, or even to Moscow. The journey is its own end, and it will not, by having no destination, any less assist the world to become what Moscow should be.
>
> Poems which have a destination, a final solution—

whether it be the enunciation of a supposed truth, or suasion to a policy, or the attainment of an end-state of consciousness, or some temporary or permanent exclusive attitude to the world, to society, or to the self, have only a subordinate value. Instead of establishing, as the best poetry does, the norms of value, they have to be judged by standards more inclusive than themselves. . . . (pp. 213–14)

Poetry with "insides," poetry which "gives most pleasure when only generally . . . understood," (p. 214) requires "receptive submission" (p. 216). T. S. Eliot's "Ash Wednesday" is a good example of poetry with insides. To grasp this poem requires

movements of exploration and resultant ponderings. . . . These very movements . . . are the very life of the poem. In these searchings for meanings of a certain sort its being consists. The poem is a quest, and its virtue is not in anything said by it, or in the way in which it is said, or in a meaning which is found, or even in what is passed by in the search." (pp. 216–17)

In the closing pages of the book, Richards works up to his final eulogy of poetry: it is up to the poet to reconstitute the order of mind dissolved in the modern novel. With the traditional accounts of knowledge gone, with the recognition that all knowledge is a vast mythology, poetry assumes its true and tremendous importance.

There is little in the foregoing summary which seems to fulfill the promise of the valuable theory of literature which I have claimed may be found in *Coleridge*. It is true that in the

33

characterization of the coadunative imagination, in the explanation of the way in which a distinction of the four senses of "nature" clarifies the seeming opposition between the projective and realistic accounts, and in the suggestion of a solution to the conflict between fact and value, I have gone beyond a simple summary of *Coleridge on Imagination* to offer interpretations of the work. At all points, however, I have preserved Richards' basic presentation. The first impression one receives is that the book is a hodgepodge of poorly integrated insights. Such an impression is only intensified by a closer reading. I have omitted from my summary the distracting quotations heading each chapter, the puzzling parable from Chuang Tzu appearing at the end of "The Boundaries of the Mythical," and most of the irritating fluctuations in Richards' position. How, for example, are we to know whether or not Richards feels that imaginative poetry is preferable to fanciful poetry? We find him asserting, at one point, that though Coleridge usually viewed imagination as being of greater value, this is not the proper way to conceive it: "Imagination . . . can be shown in trivial examples. And Fancy can be shown in important matters" (pp. 91–92). But four pages later he claims that Coleridge's uniting of his psychology and his theory of value "does more justice to the unity of mental process" (p. 96). Or how are we to know whether or not the projective and coadunative imaginations are really different? He claims, in one place, that "projection is not enough to make a passage imaginative [in a coadunative sense]" (p. 110), but eleven pages later uses the coadunation involved in projection of meaning to explain how fanciful poetry can delight through its meter.

Such a clutter of changing views is characteristic of Richards' later works. But perhaps he should not be criticized for this. The distinction which Richards draws in *Coleridge* between a fact of mind and doctrine suggests that the material presented

there is to be understood not as doctrine but as fact of mind—
that this work itself is an instrument to think *with,* but not
about. If this is so, its contradictions and clutter would be
of more worth than any clear presentation.

This obscurantist suggestion is hardly satisfactory, however,
and were this the only use to which *Coleridge* might be put, it
would not merit the elaborate attention I have already devoted
to it. There is a way of looking at *Coleridge* which renders it
much more intelligible and interesting. The key to this approach
lies in adherence to the Platonic maxim, "Keep things in their
proper places," which Richards himself urges us to adopt in a
late essay.[4] Following this maxim in the way which I shall
presently illustrate does not eliminate all the difficulties of the
book, though it does help with many. *Coleridge* is close enough
to the earlier works for there still to be vestiges of the misleading metaphors appearing in them. Such metaphors, for instance, give rise to the tension between the two themes developed in "The Boundaries of the Mythical," where poetry is
seen both to solve and to deepen the conflict between science
and value. Though a full account of the backgrounds of the
themes must be delayed until Chapter 5, I might note here that
the reduction of all experiences to impulses underlies the assimilation of poetry and other values, and early versions of the
emotive-referential distinction underlie the rift between science
and value. Thus, the theme of conflict between science and
poetry leans heavily upon frameworks adopted in Richards'
earlier works.

In *Coleridge* Richards does not keep in their proper places
the widely divergent interests of the various sorts of individuals
concerned with art—the interests, for instance, of the aesthetician, the critic, the reader, and the moralist. Richards' con-

4. *Speculative Instruments,* p. 52.

fusion of these interests is not new in *Coleridge,* though it perhaps reaches its high point in that work. Here, for instance, are the questions he cites in *Principles* as being those which the *critic* should answer:

> What gives the experience of reading a certain poem its value? How is this experience better than another? Why prefer this picture to that? In which ways should we listen to music so as to receive the most valuable moments? Why is one opinion about works of art not as good as another? . . . What *is* a picture, a poem, a piece of music? How can experiences be compared? What is value? (pp. 5–6)

In a much later work, Richards seems to recognize the danger of such confusions:

> But talk about poems may have all sorts of purposes behind it: social, suasive, literary, comparative, analytic, scientific. . . . Behind the words, "literary criticism," we will find at least as many different studies with diverse aims as was the case with "Grammar" . . . . Meanwhile confusion between these aims is the chief source of controversies about general critical theory.[5]

It seems, however, that he was not conscious of this pitfall at the time of writing *Coleridge.*

The confusion emerges almost immediately in Chapter I of *Coleridge.* The critic, Richards suggests, should be reflective. Coleridge's great merit as a critic "is the strenuous persistence with which he reflected philosophically upon criticism. Is there not something a little ridiculous in saying, 'What a fine critic!

5. *Interpretation in Teaching* (London, 1938), p. 369.

What a pity he thought so hard about poetry!'?" (p. 5) We wonder whether Coleridge is great because of his thoughts about poetry or because of his thoughts about the criticism of poetry. Is he great as a critic or great as an aesthetician?

More distinctions are flaunted as Chapter I unfolds: study of Coleridge will enable us to understand ourselves, to understand Coleridge's critical theories, to understand Coleridge's criticism, to understand the nature of poetry. Confusions of these aims are repeated throughout the book, reaching their peak in the chapter "Good Sense." Indeed, Richards blunts the distinctions so frequently that one is truly surprised, in the last few pages of the book, to find him explicitly drawing a distinction between the value of poetry and the value of the study of poetry. But the change is short-lived. The "study of poetry" is quickly equated with the "study of the modes of language," and thence

> the more traditional subjects of criticism, Coleridge's differentation of imagination from fancy, and his still abstruser ponderings on objectification and the living word, unite with the analysis of the ambiguities and confusions that are overt or latent in all cases of metaphor . . . to form one study. (p. 232)

Although a concentration on these confusions may at first intensify our disappointment with the work, it is obvious that awareness of Richards' own shifting focus may afford us an approach to a more positive evaluation. Indeed, the three areas where the confusions seem most serious—Richards' account of projection, his analysis of good sense, and his treatment of the realizing intuition—take on new significance when we envisage the possibility of unannounced changes in perspective.

37

The first area of confusion concerns Richards' account of projection, a concept central to Richards' discussion in *Coleridge*. He uses it in Chapters III and VIII to characterize the operation of the imagination and the values that accrue from this operation. The secondary imagination projects and balances values, and it is through this balance that poetry accomplishes the resolution of the conflict between science and value. We sense a conflation of interests here. While the aesthetician is concerned both with the nature of the imaginative experience and its relation to other activities, he is, in the latter concern, adopting the role of the moralist. This conflation is not, however, nearly so distressing as Richards' failure to distinguish this sort of projection, which is of primary interest to the aesthetician, from that which primarily concerns the reader or critic. The projection which Richards describes in Chapter VI refers to the way in which the reader or critic regards the words of a poem; it does not characterize the nature and value of the imaginative experience. To some extent, it is true, Richards keeps these two sorts of projection separate. But sometimes he does not. He introduces his account of the coadunative imagination (of primary concern to the aesthetician) with an example of the projective imagination (of primary concern to the reader or critic); he uses the coadunation of meanings in projection, as we have seen above, to explain the metrical appeal of fanciful poetry.

A clear separation of the different uses clarifies some problems encountered in Chapters IV and V. In Chapter V, for example, Richards suggests that coadunatively imaginative poetry will typically be read as projectively imaginative (p. 110). In his accounts in Chapter IV of the "apprehension" and "mutual modification" of the parts of a work's meanings, however, the coadunative imagination clearly relies for its effect on a sharp distinction between the meaning of a part and its effects, that is, on non-projection of meaning (pp. 88–90). We can solve this puzzle if we understand the "non-projection" of meaning in the discussion of the coadunative imagination, not as a reference to the way in which poetry is read or regarded, but as an account of the way in which the experience of the poem actually develops.

The second area of serious confusion centers around Richards' views on the use of theory. In the earlier chapters of *Coleridge,* Richards frequently urges his readers to value theory not as the end of a search but as a tool to facilitate the search. In this vein he notes that his own interpretations of Coleridge are to be valued for their stimulation of interest in problems of criticism, that Coleridge's theories are to be used as instruments for exploring the nature of poetry, and that the descriptions of fancy and imagination are justified solely by their illumination of different experiences (pp. xii–xiv, 21, 85). In Chapter VI, Richards explicitly develops this theme, and it is here that we find him most flagrantly confusing different people's interests.

At times in this chapter, Richards' advocacy of an instrumental use of theory amounts to his urging the critic or reader to adhere to rules—conscious or unconscious—to ensure the full understanding, and hence proper evaluation, of a poem. Thus Richards quotes Coleridge's suggestion that a line is bad because it violates the language of good sense—that is, because it conveys incongruous images and confounds cause and effect. Later he criticizes Coleridge's use of good sense in his objection to Wordsworth's *Ode* (pp. 124, 130–37). Such a use of theory underlies Richards' discussion of the microscopic power of theory, which represents the merits of a passage as a necessary prelude to, but not a replacement for, the "act of living" which judges it. At some points in the chapter, however, Richards uses "theory" to refer to a device of primary concern to the

39

aesthetician, such as the distinction between the imagination and fancy. Such a theory may illuminate the nature of poetry or the human mind, but it is difficult to see how it would be used to examine and describe the merits of a particular passage. Use of the second sort of theory should perhaps be related to use of the first. Critical theory (how images should or should not be taken, for example) illuminates the poetic work for the reader. One justification of the study of the theory of poetry (Coleridge's theory of imagination, for example) is the aid it affords the reader in dealing with poetry. (Such a justification would explain how Richards can use his lengthy discussion of Coleridge's critical obtuseness in interpreting Wordsworth's *Ode* to raise the question: what good is Coleridge's theory about poetry if it leads to blunders such as these? [p. 137]) But Richards' confusion of the two sorts of theory merely renders the task of relating them more difficult.

The third instance in which Richards most obviously ignores the different interests impinging on poetry is in his use of the concept of the realizing intuition. There is scarcely a facet of his argument, whether it concerns the problems of developing a theory of poetry, the reading of imaginative poetry, or the value of this poetry, in which the "coalescence of subject and object" characteristic of the realizing intuition does not play a central role. Here are just a few examples. Coleridge caught and recorded his "realizing acts of intuition" concerning the *nature of poetry* in his metaphysical machinery; Richards will try to use it for the same purpose (p. 21). The coalescence of subject and object underlies *imaginative reading*. Unless one goes through this "realizing intuition," in which he comes both to make and know himself, he will not uncover the growth of mind, the self-creation and self-realization, which develops in such reading (p. 69). The realizing intuition underlies the *identification* of a poetic passage. The link is found in the concept of freedom, which is the basis of the realizing intuition. The individual freely makes himself in knowing himself. But, as we saw in the summary above, it is through freedom that the imagination identifies an instance of itself (p. 98). The realizing intuition *mediates* the conflict between science and value. This conflict is resolved by a return to a fact of mind, which Richards calls at one point the "immediate self-consciousness in the imaginative moment" (p. 162).

Richards attempts at times to distinguish these different uses. For example, in Chapter III, he explicitly distinguishes introspection from both the realizing intuition and the "mode of self-creation" which Coleridge uses to divide the imagination from the fancy (p. 49). This would seem to indicate a distinction between the realizing intuition and the reading or study of poetry, but Richards undercuts his own distinction in the conclusion to this chapter, where he stresses the usefulness of Coleridge's theory of the mind (presumably his views on realizing intuition) as an instrument for examining poetry (p. 69). In fact, realizing intuition seems to be a convenient glue which Richards uses to hold together various aspects of his theory. In Chapter III, where the concept is supposedly explicated, none of the notions introduced to clarify it remains fixed. It is not clear, for instance, whether the realizing intuition is the *same* as the first postulate of philosophy, or is the *source* of this postulate. Just as unsatisfactory are the abrupt transitions from section to section in this chapter, with no indications of relationships between the sections. Richards starts his discussion of the imagination with coalescence, then, for no apparent reason, remarks: "And here Coleridge's separation of a Primary from a Secondary Imagination may be considered" (p. 57). Furthermore, there is no indication of the relationship between coalescence and later themes, such as the projective imagination or the senses of "nature." Richards seems impatient with Coleridge's hurriedly developed "metaphysical machinery" and anxious to get on to other topics. No clarification of realizing intuition is found here or elsewhere, I think, because there is none which Richards could offer. The term is ambiguous, meaning one thing, for instance, in Richards' discussion of the nature of an imaginative reading and another in his discussion of the value of poetry. One finds, then, three clear examples of Richards' confusion of different interests in poetry—his account of projection, his analysis of good sense, and his treatment of the realizing intuition.

I have offered one basic criticism of *Coleridge on Imagination* but many others could be developed. Richards is maddeningly vague. How are we to relate his analysis of imagination in terms of the "parts" of a meaning to his strictures against "unwary abstraction" of elements of the whole poem? (pp. 87–88; 119) What is this mutual enlivening of parts? How can an interpretation of one part determine the interpretation of another? How is the coadunation of parts related to the growth of the mind, which Richards cites as the result of reading imaginatively? What is meant by science's "complete" as opposed to poetry's "partial" control over our actions? How can poetry establish norms? Such basic questions can, however, best be answered by viewing them in the context of Richards' work as a whole; I shall not attempt to answer them now or raise further questions of this sort before examining his other writings.

It is time, rather, to use my primary criticism to restructure Richards' presentation in *Coleridge*. What happens when, in reading the book, we separate the divergent interests of the different sorts of individuals concerned with poetry? I shall not attempt to deal with the interests of everyone concerned

with the poetic process. Archeologists and sociologists, for instance, may have very special interests in poetry which will not
receive my attention. I shall be concerned with all the most
obvious remaining candidates—readers, critics, moralists, and
aestheticians—except poets. As the exception may seem surprising, it is worth noting that, although Coleridge develops his
account of the imagination in terms of the characteristics of the
poet "described in ideal perfection,"[6] Richards uses this account primarily to elucidate the poem as it is grasped by the
critic or reader, used by the moralist, or studied by the aesthetician. In the central chapters of *Coleridge,* devoted to the distinction between imagination and fancy, meter, and good sense,
Richards is always absorbed in the problems that arise from
the reading or criticizing of literature, never in those arising
from its creation. Even in the later chapters, where he deals
directly with the "mythopoeic" power, his concern is more with
the "re-creation" of the fact of mind by those who read or study
literature, than with its original creation. Richards probably
thinks that those who read correctly reproduce the phases of
mental activity originally involved in writing. But he never
argues this point and does not seem concerned to do so. We
shall find this de-emphasis of the poet characteristic of much
of his other later writing.

The peculiarity of the aesthetician's interest deserves men-
tion. He has his own special interest in art, which I might characterize as the analysis of the nature and value of the aesthetic
experience. Indirectly, however, he is concerned with the interests of all the other parties involved in the artistic process.
To formulate an aesthetic theory, he must harmonize these
interests with his own. The situation is reminiscent of Plato's

6. See I. A. Richards, "Introduction," *The Portable Coleridge,* ed.
I. A. Richards (New York, 1950), pp. 45–46.

depiction of reason in the human soul: reason has its own special interests, but its job is not simply to secure these interests, but to harmonize them with those of passion and appetite in order to serve the whole individual.[7] With this point in mind, I should modify my earlier claim that the projection in Chapter VI was not the aesthetician's concern but the reader's or critic's, to state that this projection is also the aesthetician's concern, though only as harmonizer of the various interests that converge upon poetry.

A number of schemes could be developed to present a theory of literature in which different concerns with literature would be recognized and harmonized. I have chosen to accomplish this end by distinguishing commerce with the literary work into three phases: activity, approach, and outcome. An analysis of the *activity* of reading illuminates the nature and value of the literary experience, and thus answers the specific demands of the aesthetician. An analysis of the *approach* to the work—particularly of the grounds for discriminating adequate from inadequate approaches and of evaluation—answers the demands of the reader and critic. Finally, an analysis of the *outcome* of reading uncovers the relationships between the literary experience and other experiences, and thus meets the demands of the moralist. If these three phases are discovered to be mutually supporting, the more general task of the aesthetician will have been accomplished: he will have developed a theory of literature.

When read with this scheme in mind, Richards' *Coleridge on Imagination* suggests the following literary theory, which is very different from that attributed to Richards by the average critic of Chapter 1: poetic language is language which occasions mul-

7. See H. W. B. Joseph, *Essays in Ancient and Modern Philosophy* (Oxford, 1935), ch. 3.

tiple interpretation. The comprehension of any utterance, except the most rigid prose, probably demands consideration of alternate interpretations. To comprehend non-poetic language, however, the reader must arrive at a single interpretation, while to comprehend poetic language he must accept multiple interpretations. Such acceptance shifts the reader's interest away from what is said by the utterance to the process of utterance itself. The conceptual frameworks supporting the different interpretations and the purposes underlying the establishment of these frameworks become indirect objects of concern as the interpreter becomes absorbed in contrasting the various meanings which he uncovers. In the development of alternate readings, there is, then, a balancing of purposes. This dynamic balance constitutes the living suspension of action, the growth and self-realization which is the unique value to be gained from reading poetry.

Such valuable experiences arise only when the reader approaches the poem as an entity with its own integrity, not as a mere instrument for the transmission of a message; as a living thing, not an inanimate object. Just as he realizes that his understanding of a person's nature is not exhaustive in any single encounter, so the reader must realize that worthwhile experiences will not develop in reading poetry unless he approaches the poem from many different perspectives. These perspectives are indicated by the critical rules which underlie correct readings. Since they indicate ways of approaching the work, adherence to such rules is requisite for proper evaluation. But the rules in no way exhaust the poem; they merely lead the reader to it.

The intrinsic value of poetry lies, as I have indicated, in the way in which it forces the reader to become absorbed in the purposes underlying his interpretations. This absorption is uniquely rewarding in itself, but it also explains the instrumental value of poetry. A concern with purposes should permeate all human activities. It is the propaedeutic to any advance in spheres as diverse as science and morality. The great value of poetry derives from the fact that, by emphasizing what is common to these disciplines, it mediates their conflict.

No part of the theory of literature sketched above is explicitly developed in *Coleridge on Imagination,* but the book is replete with hints of it. The relevance of the multiple interpretations of a poetic utterance and the self-realization involved in reading poetry may be seen in Richards' description of the imagination in Chapter IV, while the importance of balancing purposes may be found in his description of wisdom in Chapter VIII. The need for viewing the poem as an entity with an integrity of its own is indicated in Richards' description of the animating force of the projective imagination in Chapter V and in his approval of Coleridge's likening words in poetry to living parts of a plant in Chapter IX, while the instrumental function of theory and the impossibility of basing evaluation directly upon it is outlined in his chapter on good sense. Finally, the instrumental value of poetry in lessening the conflict between science and value is urged in Chapters VIII and IX.

Especially noteworthy is the way in which Richards' varied uses of the realizing intuition support the theory. Reading poetry involves a shift from concentration on what is said to the process of utterance, that is, a move from doctrine to the fact of mind. The resulting involvement with purposes represents the synthesis of knowing and doing characteristic of the realizing intuition. The grounding of the realizing intuition in freedom, and the claim that in reading, the imagination "re-cognizes" itself, appear in the analysis of the approach to the poem. The reader must view it as a living, freely developing being. Finally, the mediating function of poetry is grounded in that characteristic of non-poetic activities which is shared by poetry. This characteristic is discovered in the return to the fact of mind

from which the different activities spring, and in the self-knowledge consequently afforded.

Although the theory I have outlined evidently is adumbrated
in *Coleridge on Imagination,* it can be fully understood only
with the help of Richards' other writings. In the next three chapters I shall turn to these other works—early and late—to fill in
what is an incomplete but tantalizing sketch. Each of these
chapters will be devoted to one of the three phases of commerce with the poem—activity, approach, and outcome—outlined above. Let us turn first, then, to a closer examination of
Richards' views on the activity of reading poetry.

3

The Activity of Reading Poetry: Emotive Language and Metaphor

A complete systematization must take the form of such an adjustment as will preserve free play to every impulse, with entire avoidance of frustration. In any equilibrium of this kind . . . we are experiencing beauty.

As we realize beauty we become more fully ourselves the more our impulses are engaged. If, as is sometimes alleged, we are the whole complex of our impulses, this fact would explain itself. Our interest is not canalized in one direction rather than another. It becomes ready instead to take any direction we choose. This is the explanation of that detachment so often mentioned in artistic experience. We become impersonal or disinterested.[1]

The more minutely and imaginatively we examine the process by which an utterance forms—and, correspondingly, is understood—the more fully we realize how interdependent WHAT and HOW here are. This unity of content

1. C. K. Ogden, I. A. Richards, and James Wood, *The Foundations of Aesthetics* (London, 1922), pp. 75, 78.

and form, of spirit and letter, of intuition and expression, is, of course, a perennial theme of criticism and of poetry itself.

> O body swayed to music, o brightening glance,
> How can we know the dancer from the dance!

The most important thing about poetry . . . is that it exemplifies this interdependence, this unity. It strives to be exemplary in this; it is our exemplar—for that kind of mutual and just control of part by part which is health.

Poetry offers, with the widest scope, exercise in choices. Prophecy demands, with equally wide scope, the exercise of choice. They are both concerned—acknowledged or unacknowledged—with legislation: what to feel, to do, to be, or to try to be.[2]

Thirty-eight years separate these two statements, the first of which appears in Richards' earliest published work and the second in one of his most recent writings on the nature of poetry. The two works differ markedly in purpose. *Foundations of Aesthetics* outlines sixteen theories of beauty, "not to bring theories into opposition with one another, but by distinguishing them to allow to each its separate sphere of validity" (pp. 5–6). "The Future of Poetry" is a plea for poets and readers to "wake up" and realize the tremendous potential of poetry *(Screens,* p. 127). The former work has a stylistic clarity completely absent from the latter; yet there is an evident similarity between the statements. The synaesthetic equilibrium of impulses which leads to our development through detachment becomes the recognition of an exemplary interdependence of

2. I. A. Richards, "The Future of Poetry," *Screens,* pp. 123–24, 126.

elements which offers exercise in choices. In each passage a unified balance is related to the individual's growth. In this chapter I shall develop the theme common to both passages by examining Richards' varied statements on the activity of reading poetry. If we grasp Richards' basic insight here, his views on the approach to the poem and the outcome of reading follow easily.

One naturally looks to Richards' discussions of emotive language to understand his views on the nature of poetic language, since throughout his works he has held that poetry is a paradigm of the emotive use of language. In *The Meaning of Meaning* (1923) poetry is called the "supreme form of emotive language" (p. 271), and as late as 1949 Richards states in "Emotive Language Still" that "emotive ingredients of meaning are . . . responsible for most of the work done by the language of poetry."[3] The investigation is complicated, however, by the fact that Richards uses the concept of emotive language in three different ways. He characterizes it first as language which is used non-referentially; second, as language which arouses attitudes; and third, as language which occasions a special sort of interpretation. I believe that the third characterization, which actually incorporates elements of the other two, most accurately captures what Richards intends to convey by emotive language as exemplified in poetry. This description may best be understood, however, against the background of the first two, which, though weakened by association with his psychological theory of poetry, are presented with greater clarity. The first two descriptions will be considered here; the third will be treated in later sections.

3. *Yale Review, 39* (1949), 112–13.

Richards distinguishes referential from non-referential uses of language in *The Meaning of Meaning,* and although there are minor changes in his accounts of the different uses in later works, the general outlines are clear from this early work. Besides the strictly symbolic or referential use of language, Richards delineates four functions of language in *The Meaning of Meaning:* the expression of the attitude of the speaker toward his audience; the expression of his attitude toward the things to which he is referring; the expression of his intention or the effects which he is trying to produce; and the "support of reference" (pp. 357–60). By this last function, Richards means the "ease or difficulty" with which the speaker refers to the thing referred to. He illuminates this use by citing two sentences: "I seem to remember ascending Mount Everest" and "I went up Everest," claiming that, on occasion, they may have the same reference and "owe their dissimilarity solely to degrees of difficulty in recalling this uncommon experience" (p. 359).

In *Practical Criticism* Richards introduces the familiar quartet of language functions: sense, feeling, tone, and intention. "Sense," "feeling," and "tone" are nothing more than new names for the "strictly symbolic use," "the expression of attitude toward the things referred to," and "expression of attitude toward the audience" of *The Meaning of Meaning.* The "expression of intention" of that work, however, is broadened in *Practical Criticism* to include unconscious as well as conscious aims or effects (pp. 181–82). In later works Richards sometimes alters the early picture by regrouping these language functions, as in *Mencius on the Mind,*[4] where he contrasts with

4. *Mencius on the Mind, Experiments in Multiple Definition,* New York, 1932.

sense all the non-referential uses taken together as "gesture" (p. 98). Occasionally he introduces a new category, as in "Fifteen Lines from Landor,"[5] where he distinguishes metaphoric senses of words from literal senses *(Speculative Instruments, p. 184).* The latest and perhaps most exhaustive description of the different uses of language may be found in "Towards a Theory of Comprehension,"[6] originally published in 1952 as "Towards a Theory of Translating."[7] Here Richards distinguishes seven linguistic functions: indicating, characterizing, realizing, valuing, influencing, controlling, and purposing. Some of *The Meaning of Meaning* categories are reflected in this picture. Thus the strictly symbolic use is represented by indicating and characterizing, that is, pointing to things and making statements about the things pointed to; support of reference is echoed in the realizing function; and valuing seems to be the counterpart of the old attitude toward referent. In these areas Richards' accounts are more subtle but not markedly different from the earlier discussions. There is, for instance, besides the explicit division of the strictly symbolic uses, a recognition and distinction of two sorts of realization—a "lively, concrete, actualized presence" and a "cognizance of implications and consequences" *(Speculative Instruments,* p. 32)—and the citation of several different ranges of valuing—not only the attitudes captured in expressions such as "good," "bad," "right," "wrong," "important," and "trivial," but the ranges of love and hate, desire and fear, belief and disbelief (p. 35). The functions of influencing, controlling, and purposing, however, which Richards describes in colloquial terms such as "would change or keep as it

5. *Speculative Instruments,* pp. 181–97.
6. Ibid., pp. 17–38, esp. pp. 26–38.
7. *Studies in Chinese Thought,* ed. Arthur F. Wright (Chicago, 1953), pp. 247–62.

is," "manages, directs, runs, administers itself," and "seeks, pursues, tries, endeavours to be or to do" (p. 26), seem to be new departures.

Actually the new functions are foreshadowed in the development of the original function of intention. Having enlarged this function in *Practical Criticism* to include unconscious aims, Richards comments in that work that it is not really on all fours with the other functions (p. 182n.). In an appendix he notes that intention "controls the relations among themselves of the other three functions" (p. 356), and at one point he characterizes the "aim" of the poem as "the whole state of mind, the mental condition, which in another sense *is* the poem. Roughly the collection of impulses which shaped the poem originally, to which it gave expression, and to which, in an ideally susceptible reader it would again give rise" (p. 204n.).

Richards' inclusion of intention among uses of language is confusing. Certainly it is important that an utterance be properly interpreted, but it is highly misleading to call this proper interpretation, the intention of the utterance, a "function" or "use" of language. We shall see below that intention, understood as the supposed aim of an utterance, plays an important role in Richards' analysis of the *comprehension* of the utterance. The comprehension of an utterance also is paramount in Richards' description of controlling in "Towards a Theory of Comprehending" as the "management, control, or administration of comprehending" *(Speculative Instruments,* p. 35), which, in behalf of purposing, adjudicates between the various functions of language. But however acceptable such analyses may prove to be, this confusion between the use and comprehension of language vitiates Richards' first characterization of emotive language as "language used non-referentially."

Even if those uses which more properly concern the process

of comprehending were discounted (and, interestingly, intention is missing from the list of "parts" of the meaning of an utterance in *Coleridge* [p. 88]), the characterization of emotive language as "language used non-referentially" fails because it covers only the use of language by a speaker and not its reception by a listener. In *The Meaning of Meaning* Richards claims that "under the emotive function are included both the expression of emotions, attitudes, moods, intentions, etc., in the speaker, and their communication, *i.e.,* their evocation in the listener" (p. 258). Without a specification of the listener's response to emotively used language, it is not clear that such language actually *evokes* emotions, attitudes, and moods, and is not simply interpreted referentially by the listener as *indicating the presence of* such emotions, attitudes, and moods in the speaker. The possibility of the latter sort of interpretation is explicitly recognized by Richards in *The Meaning of Meaning* when he suggests that in hearing a sentence

> we are confronted by . . . at least two sign-situations. One is interpreted from symbols to reference and so to referent; the other is interpreted from verbal signs to the attitude, mood, interest, purpose, desire, and so forth of the speaker, and thence to the situation, circumstances and conditions in which the utterance is made. (p. 356)

Again, in *Practical Criticism* he distinguishes the "two important senses in which we can 'understand' the feeling of a passage. We can either just ourselves *undergo* the same feeling or we can *think of* the feeling" (p. 331).

Richards' second characterization of emotive language as language which arouses attitudes, as opposed to language which arouses thoughts, obviates such a referential interpretation. The most complete description of such arousal is found in those chapters of *Principles of Literary Criticism* where Richards sketches and elaborates his psychological theory. Any experience, he states, may be described in terms of impulses in the experiencer's nervous system—particularly in his brain. He justifies this claim in two steps. First, every bit of overt behavior is preceded by a "preliminary organization" in the mental state of the actor (p. 108). Second, "that the mind is the nervous system, or rather a part of its activity, has long been evident" (p. 83). An impulse is a process occasioned by a stimulus and usually ending in a response, in the course of which a mental event may occur. Richards replaces the traditional analyses of mental experience in terms of thought, feeling, and volition with analyses in terms of the causes, characters, and consequences of these mental events (chs. 11–15).

The stimulus for an impulse is typically some object or event perceived by the individual, and its course is immediately affected by the condition of the experiencer's other impulses. "When hungry and when replete we respond differently to the stimulus of a smell of cooking. A change in the wind unnoticed by the passengers causes the captain to reduce sail" (pp. 86–87). An impulse does not worm its way through the set of impulses it meets "as through a piece of cheese." In fact, "stimuli are only received if they serve some need of the organism and the form which the response to them takes depends only in part upon the nature of the stimulus, and much more upon what the organism 'wants' " (p. 87). Mental events have, then, two sources, one external and one internal. So far as an impulse remains undistorted by the internal source, a mental event occurring in its course affords knowledge of the stimulus; so far as it is distorted, such a mental event does not afford knowledge.

Another influence on the course of an impulse is the other impulses aroused simultaneously with it. Richards uses this factor to analyze the character and consequence of a mental event. The character of a mental event, its "feeling" (which may or may not be introspectible as an emotion or feeling, depending on whether or not the mental event is conscious), is confusingly represented by Richards as a characteristic of the stimulus itself, as a characteristic of the response to the stimulus, and as a function of the convergence of different stimuli (chs. 12, 13). The consequence of a mental event is normally an action. Where there is a convergence of a great number of different impulses, however, the impulses tend to balance one another, and the responses which might have occurred had the impulses remained isolated are replaced by "attitudes" or "imaginal and incipient activities or tendencies to action (p. 112). Utilizing a substitution theory of language which I shall outline in the next section, Richards claims that words similarly arouse attitudes, as opposed to thoughts, when the impulses stemming from them become distorted (ch. 16). Language used to refer to states of affairs, no less than language used to express attitudes, may arouse attitudes instead of thoughts. Such a use of language Richards calls a use of reference "for the sake of" attitudes or emotions.[8]

The trouble with this theory is, of course, that Richards never makes clear how these attitudes come about. Neither description of the distortion of impulses—that in terms of the existing conditions in the organism or that in terms of the interaction of impulses received conjointly—is really satisfactory. The first demands too great a similarity in the needs and interests of different experiencers. The second—which is the basis for the synaesthetic experience described at the beginning of this

8. *Meaning of Meaning,* p. 259; *Principles,* p. 267.

chapter—merely underscores the obscurity in both accounts
of distortion. What, precisely, *is* an impulse, distorted or otherwise? How can one impulse distort another? Instead of trying
to answer these questions Richards delights in offering us pictures to assist our thought.

> Imagine a circle or sphere constantly bombarded by
> minute particles (stimuli). Within the sphere may be
> pictured complex mechanisms continually changing for
> reasons having nothing to do with the external stimuli.
> These mechanisms by opening little gateways select
> which of the stimuli shall be allowed to come in and take
> effect. So far as the subsequent convulsions are due to
> the nature of the impacts and to lingering effects of im-
> pacts which have accompanied similar impacts in the
> past, the convulsions are referential. So far as they are
> due to the independent motions of the internal mecha-
> nisms themselves, reference fails.[9]

The impulse theory provides no real explanation of the genesis
or nature of attitudes. It simply assures us that Richards believes them to be central to the reading of poetry.

Richards' second characterization of emotive language suffers from the same weaknesses as his first—vagueness and incompleteness. We are not told clearly how attitudes arise in
reading poetry, and no justice is done to the expressive as opposed to the evocative aspect of emotive language. Neither the
description of emotive language as language used non-referen-

9. *Principles,* p. 263.

tially nor its description as language arousing attitudes promises, then, to illuminate the nature of poetic language. The situation is quite the reverse with Richards' third account, in which emotive language is characterized as requiring a different kind of interpretation than referential language. Though incorporating facets of the other two accounts, this characterization avoids their difficulties and has far-reaching implications. Unfortunately, the conception is never fully developed by Richards in any single place, but must be gathered from hints scattered throughout his writings. Thus it stands in much greater need of elucidation than did the first two conceptions.

My characterization of this third conception of emotive language as language which demands a special sort of interpretation suggests two major questions. First, what are the differences in the two sorts of interpretation? Second, what forces an individual to interpret in a special fashion? The second question I shall defer until Chapter 4, where I consider the poetic process from the critic's and reader's perspectives. Here I shall concentrate on distinguishing the different sorts of interpretation.

As a preliminary to characterizing the special sort of interpretation occasioned by emotive language, we need to examine the model Richards uses to discuss the interpretation of *any* utterance, the "context theory of meaning" first presented in *The Meaning of Meaning*. This theory is developed in terms of the "triangle of reference" introduced early in that work to aid in the analysis of the "strictly symbolic" use of language (p. 12, my italics). The basis of this claim lies in the close rela- strictly symbolically are the communication, recording, supporting, and organizing of *thoughts*. Nevertheless, we often claim that "symbols record *events* and communicate *facts*" (p. 12, my italics). The basis of this claim lies in the close relation of the three distinct elements involved in strictly symbolic meaning: the symbol (word), the speaker's or hearer's thought ("reference"), and the situation referred to ("referent"). There is a causal relation (called "symbolization") between the symbol and the speaker's or hearer's thought. The symbol directs the hearer's thought toward some situation; the direction of the speaker's thought causes him to choose a certain symbol. Between the speaker's or hearer's thought and the situation toward which it is directed there is also a "relation; more or less direct (as when we think about or attend to a coloured surface we see), or indirect" (p. 15). Richards characterizes this relation ("reference") as "causal," meaning "related through repeated association." Between the symbol and the situation referred to there is only an indirect relation through the speaker's or hearer's thought. Failure to grasp this fact, Richards claims, is a main source of the weakness of other discussions of meaning.

The causal relationships among the three elements are elaborated by reference to external and internal contexts. A context is a group of entities (external to the individual in the case of external contexts; internal, or mental, in the case of psychological contexts) whose members are related by repeated past association.

> When part of an external context recurs in experience this part is, through its linkage with a member of some psychological context, *i.e.,* of a causally connected group of mental events often widely separated in time, sometimes a sign of the rest of the external context. (pp. 145–46)

Richards elucidates the concept by reference to the well-known Pavlovian dog. The gong (part of the external context and a sign) is so linked to the psychological context (the dog's hearing, his past hearings, and his present memories connecting

59

these hearings to savorings in the dining room) that it becomes a sign of (becomes indirectly linked to, through the psychological context) savoring and being given food. The sign, then, is part of an external context which stands for missing parts of that context. The possibility and stability of signification depend upon the uniformity with which these external and psychological contexts have been associated (pp. 143–48).

Richards uses this context theory of meaning in several of his later works, each time referring his reader to the account in *The Meaning of Meaning*. In *The Philosophy of Rhetoric* a long section of the second chapter is devoted to a development of the theory; in "Towards a Theory of Comprehending," the comprehending of an utterance is characterized as "an instance of a nexus established through past occurrences of partially similar utterances in partially similar situations" *(Speculative Instruments,* p. 23); and in "The Future of Poetry" the "mutual control of the contexts . . . which give all reference and concern to whatever may be uttered" is described as one source of the strength of a passage *(Screens,* p. 121). There are, however, two significant ways in which these later accounts diverge from the earlier. First, non-referential language is given a place in the theory; second, Richards is here concerned with whole utterances rather than with words or simple phrases.

Richards does not analyze non-referential language in terms of the context theory in *The Meaning of Meaning*. On one occasion he does refer to a word as a member of the context of an attitude, but by this he means merely that it is "one of that group of symbols whose utterance would not alter the attitude" (p. 370). In *Rhetoric,* however, he seems ready to admit language used non-referentially within the context theory. He claims that the "same general theorem covers all the modes of meaning." The "extra meaning that comes in when a sentence, in addition to making a statement, is meant to be insulting," for instance, can be interpreted contextually in this way: "As the word means the missing part of its contexts and is a substitute for them, so the insulting intention may be the substitute for a kick,—the missing part of its context" (pp. 40–41). In "Emotive Language Still" he stresses the effects which emotive language has through its associated context.[10]

Rhetoric is one of Richards' most elusive works, and since he does not comment further on the topic of non-referential language, it is difficult to know how to interpret this shift. Is the analysis of non-referential uses being assimilated to that of symbolic uses because non-referential uses can be interpreted referentially—that is, as signs of the attitudes and feelings of the speaker? Or does the shift reflect a liberalization of the notion of context such that contexts may not only relate items through association but may also signal the adoption of active positions toward them? Richards' dropping of the distinction between internal and external contexts in *Rhetoric* may argue in favor of the latter interpretation, but I believe that he has the former in mind. To support my reading I might cite the paradoxical nature of the second suggestion and Richards' obvious concern with *interpretation* in this and other late works in which the context theory is used. To grasp an utterance accurately, say for the purpose of translation, one must be able to pinpoint precisely the various things done with the words in the utterance. This can be best accomplished by relating the utterance to similar utterances in which like functions were present. The relating demands that the functions be grasped symbolically, not responded to emotively. In *Interpretation in Teaching* and *How to Read a Page* Richards underscores the difference between understanding an attitude and sharing an attitude. The view that we must share an attitude to understand it Richards

10. *Yale Review, 39* (1949), 112.

labels the "belief snare," and he suggests that it is "among the most confusing and misleading things in all literary discussion."[11] His assimilation of non-referential language to the context theory of meaning by concentration on its referential interpretation does not mean that Richards feels that words never serve non-referential ends. It merely means that there is, *in interpretation,* no simple arousal of feelings and attitudes. The role of feelings and attitudes in interpretation is, we shall discover, somewhat more complex.

The second change in the context theory of meaning in Richards' later works is, as noted above, his concern with whole utterances rather than with words or simple phrases. Behind this shift lies a growing conviction that utterances are organic wholes. What starts out as a commonsensical observation concerning interpretation in *Mencius on the Mind*—that we must take "the whole tenor of . . . [a] work as a guide in interpreting each portion, however small," and thus that it is foolish to fix meanings for "scraps in isolation from the rest" (p. xiv)—becomes, in *Rhetoric* and "The Interactions of Words," the puzzling position that words have no meaning independent of the sentences in which they appear, that "a word is its interactions with other words."[12] Richards presents this position as the corrective to the "usage" doctrine, which holds that the meaning of a sentence is built up from the meanings of its words, as a wall from bricks—a doctrine which, he claims in *Rhetoric,* accounts for most of our errors in comprehension (p. 10, ch. 3).

The organic nature of all utterances seems paradoxical in light of the context theory of *The Meaning of Meaning.* Most

11. *Interpretation in Teaching,* p. 157. See also *How To Read a Page,* pp. 168–70.
12. "The Interactions of Words," *The Language of Poetry,* ed. Allen Tate, The *Mesures* Series in Literary Criticism (Princeton, 1942), p 74.

sentences we encounter are unique. But, according to the early book, meaning depends upon repeated association of similar elements; hence most sentences are meaningless, and so are their component words! Richards does note in *Rhetoric* some exceptional cases in which we legitimately build up the meaning of a phrase or sentence from its isolated words. Thus, "in the strict exposition of some highly criticized and settled science through technicalized and rigid speech, a large proportion of . . . [words] are independent. They mean the same whatever other words they are put with . . . " (p. 48). The best examples of such language are found in mathematics. "If . . . I were reading you the first few theorems of Euclid . . . you would understand, as soon as I said 'a triangle,' what the word meant . . . " (p. 49). But this is clearly an exception, and "in most prose, and more than we ordinarily suppose," (p. 50) the meaning of the word will be derived from the meaning of the sentence.

Richards may not, however, intend that his organic conception be taken literally; he refers on several occasions in *Rhetoric* to the meanings of words independent of context. He titles a chapter "The Interinanimation of Words," suggesting that there is some sort of animus belonging to words in isolation which affects their meaning in combination. He states that the meanings of words in a sentence come not only from other words present but also from "words which in part overlap in meaning. Words, for example, which we might have used instead, and, together with these, the reasons why we did not use them" (p. 63). And he singles out for discussion various senses of selected words, such as "book" and "intrinsicate" (pp. 64, 74).

Richards is attempting to emphasize two different points in adopting this exaggerated organic conception. First, he is stressing the overdetermination of meaning of most ordinary words.

The meaninglessness of a word out of context is a meaninglessness based on superabundance. A "word by itself apart from an utterance has no meaning—or rather it has too many possible meanings," he notes in *Coleridge* (p. 101). The partial meanings of a word can even be incompatible. No one, he says in *Rhetoric,* can bind the set of ideas he is developing, though each of these (the signatures to be bound and the set of ideas) is properly called a "book" (p. 74). There may be a few members of the usage school—Richards certainly feels there are—who would hold that there is a single proper meaning (sense, feeling, or tone) for each word. Undoubtedly other theorists have been insensitive to the multiplicity of meanings of words, or have lamented such multiplicity. But few would deny Richards this first point, and if his organicism serves only to stress this multiplicity, he seems to have grossly overstated his case.

The statement of his position becomes much more acceptable, however, when we realize Richards' second aim: to emphasize the "purpose" underlying every utterance. An important respect in which it is true that a word has no meaning independent of the sentence in which it appears is that a sentence is the shortest utterance in which a "purpose" is reflected. I have put quotation marks around the word "purpose" to indicate that Richards' use of the concept in this context is a rather unusual one. Unfortunately, his explicit analyses of the concept are not very helpful in clarifying this use. In "Towards a Theory of Comprehending," as we saw above, Richards treats purposing as a function of language. There he notes that this function is different from other functions in that it "never lapses; without purposing . . . which structures all activity, [there is] no utterance and no comprehending" *(Speculative Instruments,* pp. 27–28). He characterizes purposing colloquially as "seeks, pursues, tries, endeavours to be or to do," and uses it to frame questions for the translator: "How widely [do two utterances in two languages] . . . serve the same purposes, playing the same parts, within the varying activities they might occur in?" and for the interpreter: *"wherein, whereby,* and *wherefore, to what end?"* (pp. 26, 27, 28). In keeping with a point he makes in a later essay, however—"Purposing, if you ask for a theory about it . . . can hardly be made more than a puzzle. It is too central" *(Speculative Instruments,* pp. 172–73) —Richards does not here distinguish the various directions in which these activities and questions might lead. In *How to Read a Page*—a book whose "ultimate theme," he notes in a late preface, is "Purpose"[13]—he distinguishes seven senses of "purpose," (pp. 222–27) including that of a function actually served, an end envisaged, and a value achieved or envisaged. But because he bases these valuable distinctions upon an un-analyzed dichotomy of means and ends, his discussion is of little help in pinpointing the meaning of "purpose" in the lin-guistic context.

The unusual meaning comes out somewhat more clearly in some incidental observations in *How To Read a Page* and *Speculative Instruments:*

> We must remember that in this dissection [of words] we are endeavoring to divide at the joints, and where the joints are will be decided by our purpose. . . . (p. 222)

> There are areas of settled routine—much of trade, for example—where the fixed and comparatively simple structuring of the things and events to be dealt with allows of a fine practical equivalence between the languages used. . . . Here functions 1 [indicating], 2 [characterizing],

13. I. A. Richards, *How To Read a Page, A Course in Efficient Read-ing with an Introduction to a Hundred Great Words,* paperback ed. (Boston, 1959), p. 5.

and 6 [controlling] are serving a Purposing so general
that it can hide behind the ordering, 6, of what is said, 2,
about what, 1. (p. 37)

In "Toward a More Synoptic View,"[14] Richards views all
human activity (he calls it "acteevity") as purposive, as "feed-
ing-forward" goals. He describes this feed-forward in terms of
the taping of a computer: "Feed-forward, for me, names the
peculiar character of tapings which arise in the service of more
generic, more inclusive, tapings." As an example, Richards
considers an animal hunting: "There is a general very inclusive
taping: 'Search for food!' As he scents this or that possible
source, subordinate tapings are issued" (p. 121). Richards
later associates this description directly with language: ". . . language is inescapably a social acteevity which only comes into
existence with, and owes its whole character to, mutualities
among men and within communities" (p. 122).[15]

The stated relationships between purpose and the structures
determined by human agents touched on in these statements
suggest this special meaning for "purposing" of the linguistic
context: every utterance has the function of purposing because
it affirms some framework or organization of things and events.
This framework is rarely established by the utterance in question. But, as intelligible only within such a framework, and
thus dependent upon its acceptance, the utterance directly supports the framework and indirectly supports the attitudes which
underlie its establishment. In this use of "purpose" we find a
restatement of the view, earlier expressed in *Coleridge,* that all

14. *Speculative Instruments,* pp. 113–26.
15. See also Richards' very recent "The Secret of 'Feedforward,'"
Saturday Review of Literature (Feb. 3, 1968), pp. 14–17, particularly
p. 16.

our dealings with reality presuppose a structuring of influences on us in terms of our needs and interests.

Richards' work are replete with discussions of these organizational frameworks. A typical example is the contrasted pair of views of nature—realistic and projectionistic—described in *Coleridge,* which closely parallels the similar contrast between the "magical" and the "scientific" views of the universe in *Science and Poetry.* A few of his frameworks are fresh and intriguing, such as the American susceptibility to "suggestion" as opposed to the English sense of "tradition";[16] or the Chinese attitude toward the acceptability of a statement, determined by the way in which the statement fits in with accepted social practice, and not by its meeting intellectual standards.[17] Many of his frameworks, however, reflect literary or philosophic commonplaces, such as the relative weight afforded thought and feeling in the attitude of contemporary writers,[18] the contrast between Greek and Christian conceptions of love, and the differences between empiricistic and rationalistic views of knowledge.[19] However original or derivative his discussions may be, they reflect Richards' conviction that the human mind is capable of ordering its experience in many diverse ways, in accordance with different needs and interests.

Unfortunately, Richards obscures the point of these discussions by introducing many of them in the course of analyzing the different senses of words. Thus he uses one of his analyses

16. I. A. Richards, "The Changing American Mind," *Harper's Magazine, 154* (1927), 242–44.

17. I. A. Richards, *Basic in Teaching, East and West* (London, 1935), ch. 2; *Mencius,* pp. 55–56.

18. I. A. Richards, "Nineteen Hundred and Now," *Atlantic, 140* (1927), 312–15.

19. *How To Read a Page,* pp. 153–56, 191–209.

of one hundred "great" words in *How To Read a Page* as the occasion to contrast the different attitudes toward love and knowledge cited above. He justifies this procedure in an essay, "Multiple Definition," by claiming that the divisions of the senses which we afford basic words, such as "thought," "thing," and "fact," illuminate the ways in which our minds work.[20] This justification indicates that the "systematic wanderings" he discovers in his great words have only an indirect connection with the multiplicity of meanings which we have seen him stress in all words. All words are overdetermined in meaning, but a study of some words—particularly those drawn from the vocabulary of Basic English—illuminates the diverse frameworks that determine which meanings are relevant and which irrelevant. The unusual aim of his analyses of these special words (in such works as "Multiple Definition," *Mencius on the Mind,* and *How To Read a Page)* accounts in part for the looseness of the discussions. Sometimes he concentrates on various senses of these words in ordinary use, sometimes on their different uses, sometimes on recondite philosophic theories concerning concepts designated by the words; most frequently he combines these different considerations. All this renders his discussions practically worthless to the reader anxious to discover something about the way words mean or are used. However, it does not prevent these approaches from indicating, if in a rather uneven fashion, the wealth of man's different ways of organizing his environment.

The conviction that every utterance as long as a sentence but no unit smaller than a sentence serves some framework, clearly supports Richards' organicism. A particular framework shapes the speaker's choice of words for the utterance, and an implicit grasp of this framework is crucial to the interpretation

20. *Proceedings of the Aristotelian Society, 34* (1933), 39.

of the utterance by the listener. Comprehension of a sentence does not, then, consist simply in recording the various possible meanings of its component words. It involves discovery of the relevant framework and consequent choice among those possible meanings. If comprehension thus involves grasping the purpose of an utterance, words cannot be comprehended independently of sentences. But if they cannot be so comprehended, there is a sense in which they have no meaning.

The description of comprehension as a choice among different possible meanings of words under the aegis of a discovered framework represents at least a change of emphasis from the account of comprehension in *The Meaning of Meaning*. There Richards claims that the specification of the words' meanings results from the intersection of these words, not from active choice by the interpreter (chs. 5–6). He follows this pattern in *Principles,* where he notes, for example, that "a thought of 'mosquito' becomes a thought of 'mosquito there now' by combining a thought of 'thing of mosquito kind' with a thought of 'thing of there kind' and a thought of 'thing of now kind' " (p. 128). This scheme is the basis for his diagram and commentary in the chapter entitled "Analysis of a Poem," where the meaning of a line of poetry apparently results simply from the intersection of the effects of reading "Arcadia, Night, a Cloud, Pan and the Moon." No recognition is given to the reader's activity in interpretation.

The picture is completely changed in *The Philosophy of Rhetoric*. Though he uses the intersection model to account for the generation of concrete things from sorts, for example, "This bit of paper here now in my hand is a concrete particular to us so far as we think of it as paperish, hereish, nowish and in my hand" (p. 31), he repeatedly stresses the need for activity on the part of the reader in order to arrive at the meaning of an utterance:

> Inference and guesswork! What else is interpretation? How, apart from inference and skilled guesswork, can we be supposed ever to understand a writer or a speaker's thought? (p. 53)

> The senses of an author's words . . . are resultants which we arrive at only through the interplay of the interpretative possibilities of the whole utterance. In brief, we have to guess them and we guess much better when we realize we are guessing, and watch out for indications, than when we think we know. (p. 55)

> A discussion of the reasons for the choice of words . . . can become an introduction to the theory of all choices. . . . The better we understand what place words hold in our lives, the readier we shall be to admit that to think about their choice is the most convenient mode of thinking about the principle of all our choices. (p. 86)

I do not mean to suggest that before writing *The Philosophy of Rhetoric* Richards was unaware of the activity required in interpretation. One could argue that the whole of *Practical Criticism* makes just this point: "In poetry the means *are* justified by the end" (p. 194); and it requires all the reader's powers to grasp that end. Even in that work, however, Richards uses the model of a mechanistic intersection of different elements to portray the fixing of the meaning of an utterance, rather than the active combining of these elements by an interpreter. He sometimes seems on the verge of the latter analysis, but nonetheless stays within the mechanistic framework. For instance, in his discussion of the fixing of feeling in a poem, he claims:

> We only know that words are chameleon-like in their feeling, governed in an irregular fashion by their sur-

roundings. In this "psychical relativity" words may be compared with colours, but of the laws governing the effects of collocation and admixture hardly anything is known. (p. 213)

Richards' adherence to this unsatisfactory scheme may be explained in part by his limiting of the context theory, in the earlier works, to language used referentially. He obviously feels that discovery of the relevant framework is less crucial in the interpretation of such utterance. Probably more important (and explaining more clearly his adherence to the scheme in *Practical Criticism)* is his tendency to call intention a "function" of language. When intention is viewed as a facet of the utterance, the crucial need for activity is obscured.

In his later works Richards more than makes up for his early under-emphasis of the need for activity in interpretation. We have seen his changed position in *Rhetoric*. In this and in other late works he repeatedly stresses the organic character of the sentence and the skill required in interpretation.[21] Most frequently he pictures this skill as something latent within the interpreter, and the task of the teacher as one of merely supplying material for its exercise:

All that we can do is to provide opportunities for an extension and refinement of skills which are inexplicably, unimaginably and all-but-triumphantly, successful already. In the Confucian *Chung Yung* the clue to the self-completing growth of the mind is given in the aphorism:

21. See, e.g., the stress on organicism in "Responsibilities in the Teaching of English," *Speculative Instruments,* pp. 91–106; "Notes Toward an Agreement between Literary Criticism and Some of the Sciences," *Speculative Instruments,* pp. 3–16; and *How To Read a Page,* passim.

"In hewing an axe-handle, in hewing an axe-handle, the model for it is in our hand."[22]

Richards uses this aphorism—one almost as unenlightening as Coleridge's similar "all in each of all men"[23]—to help explain the obvious circularity in his practical suggestions for the improvement of comprehension. Understanding may be improved, he notes on different occasions, through graded exercises in interpretation, through translation of passages to simpler English, or through training in the multiple meanings of words.[24] Such endeavors would be useless for someone who did not in some sense possess the skill already.

Richards is himself often intrigued by a different circularity which marks the activity of interpretation. Successful interpreting involves discovery of the framework underlying an utterance. We must discover this framework from the words of the utterance, but we cannot interpret these words unless we have already projected the framework. Richards develops the point at numerous places, frequently relying on metaphoric language. In "Toward a Theory of Comprehending," for instance, he uses a Platonic metphor: the function of controlling which, as we saw above, is said to manage, control, and administer comprehending, "has to do with . . . decisions as to what it will be wise to suppose, and with what arises through these supposals. . . . Many of our most important supposals concern the nature of meaning and the connections of the sorts

22. *Interpretation in Teaching*, p. 18.
23. See *Coleridge*, pp. 98, 175.
24. *Interpretation in Teaching*, p. 11; *Speculative Instruments*, pp. 89, 102; *Interpretation in Teaching*, pp. 203–11; *How To Read a Page*, p. 44; "The Resourcefulness of Words," *Speculative Instruments*, pp. 72–77; *Interpretation in Teaching*, pp. 294–98; "From Criticism to Creation," *Times Literary Supplement, 3300* (May 27, 1965), 438–39.

of meaning with one another" *(Speculative Instruments,* p. 36). In fulfilling this function of controlling "we are guardians . . . and subject therefore to the paradox of government: that we must derive our powers, in one way or another, from the very forces which we have to do our best to control" (p. 38). In "The Future of Poetry" he draws a metaphor from communication theory: "The whole process by which possible parts [of a poem] accept, exclude, modify, mold one another to form a whole, which is only forefelt until it is found, operates both through feed-forward and feed-back *(i.e.* outcome reports as to the success or failure of tentatives in attaining ends which have been fed forward)." He elaborates the paradox: "Throughout the writing of poetry, coming events cast their shadows before; they cannot come until they are prepared for and yet . . . how . . . could the coming events determine what the preparation should be?" *(Screens,* p. 117) The interpretation, no less than the writing of poetry, demands such feed-forward and feed-back (p. 119). The moral which Richards derives from this paradoxical situation is the need for flexibility and openness on the part of the interpreter. Indeed, if the tone of Richards' later writings is largely determined by his absorption in the paradoxes of interpreting, a major theme there is his plea for openness and flexibility—that is, intelligence—in interpretation.

Thus far I have described Richards' changing views on interpretation in general and have not developed his views on the distinctive nature of the interpretation of poetic language. The special nature of such interpretation comes out most clearly in his contrast between "rigid" and "fluid" language. Sometimes all that Richards means by this contrast is the difference between an utterance whose meaning is built up in a mosaic fashion from the meanings of its component parts, and one whose underlying framework must be discovered to interpret the meanings of the parts; in other words, the distinction between statements requiring passive and those requiring active interpretation, as outlined above.[25] Sometimes, however, he seems to mean something quite different by the contrast:

> There is an important use of words—very frequent, I suggest, in poetry—which does not freeze its meanings but leaves them fluid, which does not fix an assertorial clip upon them in the way that scientific prose and factual discourse must. It leaves them free to move about and relate themselves in various ways to one another.[26]

Richards does not explicitly recognize any difference between these two distinctions of rigidity and fluidity, and on occasion presents the two concepts as extremes on a single scale ranging from mathematics to poetry.[27] There is an important difference here, however, and when we develop the implications of the two distinctions we discover Richards' most adequate differentiation between referential and emotive language, and hence his most developed views on the language of poetry.

Language which is rigid in the second sense is not necessarily rigid in the first sense. In fact, rigid language in the second sense includes all the utterances—rigid or fluid—referred to in the first distinction. A glance at the two distinctions should indicate why this is the case. In the first we learn of two ways—

25. *Interpretation in Teaching,* pp. 258, 311; *How To Read a Page,* p. 108; *Speculative Instruments,* p. 29.

26. "Poetry as an Instrument of Research," *Speculative Instruments,* p. 148.

27. *Rhetoric,* p. 48.

mosaic and organic—by which the meaning of an utterance is constituted; hence two ways in which what is being *asserted* by the utterance is discovered. But whether we discover the assertion in a passive or an active manner, we are still discovering an assertion. No matter how freely and flexibly we determine the meaning of an utterance, our interpretation eventuates in our "freezing" the meanings of the utterance into an "assertorial clip." This means, however, that the utterance is rigid in the second sense. Fluidity in the second sense designates non-assertion; in the first sense it designates one way in which we determine what a sentence asserts. It is not simply "scientific prose," but "factual discourse" as well, which must fix its meanings: not only the rigid "strict scientific" prose of *Rhetoric* but other fluid language as well.

An outstanding feature of Richards' later writings is his confusion of these two senses of "fluidity." Occasionally, the sense he has in mind is clear, as in the quotation above from "Poetry as an Instrument of Research." Much more typically, he flits back and forth from one sense to another. But however annoying the confusions may be, they provide a sort of bonus for the person attempting to interpret Richards' works. They allow him to expect and discover material relevant to the description of one sort of interpretation in works ostensibly devoted to the description of the other. Thus, although Richards remarks in *Rhetoric* that "my subject is Rhetoric rather than Poetics and I want to keep to prose which is not too far from the strict scientific" (p. 49), his confusions allow the reader to understand his many references here to poetry and its interpretation as properly (and reasonably) concerned with the special interpretation of poetic language. This is because, despite his expressed intent, his very confusions of the two senses of "fluidity" mean that many of his references *are* relevant to poetry. The interpreter can deal similarly with material from *Interpretation in Teaching* and *How To Read a Page*. It might be argued that such an approach constitutes a rewriting of Richards' views, and not an interpretation of them; I suggest, rather, that it is a necessary step to remove the obscurities of the later writings.

In Richards' descriptions of fluid, non-assertive language we have the basis of his third and most adequate characterization of emotive language, and hence the basis of his analysis of poetry. Examination of this language thus allows me to develop the hints offered at the end of my second chapter concerning Richards' views on the reading of poetry. Three related features of non-assertive language illuminate its nature: it has multiple meanings; it is untranslatable; it is complete.

The first feature is found in *Coleridge* where Richards emphasizes the multiplicity of meanings which arise from the reading of the imaginative passage from *Venus and Adonis:*

> Look! how a bright start shooteth from the sky
> So glides he in the night from Venus' eye.

Richards remarks:

> Here . . . the more the image is followed up, the more links of relevance between the units are discovered. . . . The separable meanings of each word, *Look!* (our surprise at the meteor, hers at his flight), *star* (a light-giver, an influence, a remote and uncontrollable thing) . . . *glides* (not rapidity only, but fatal ease, too) . . .—all these separable meanings are here brought into one. (p. 83)

> After apprehending how *a bright star shooteth from the sky* we respond to Adonis' gliding otherwise. And reciprocally the development of Feeling (and Tone) from

76

bright star shooteth is modified by our knowledge, for example, that Adonis is going to his death. Latent possibilities in it are called out. (pp. 89–90)

In Imagination . . . in the ideal case, all the possible characters of any part are elicited and a place found for them, consentaneous with the rest, in the whole response. (p. 92)

This inclusion of all the different meanings of the words of the utterance in its final meaning is reminiscent of some of Richards' earlier views. It recalls the synaesthetic equilibrium described in the passage quoted from *The Foundations of Aesthetics* at the head of this chapter, where "free play" is given to all impulses. We are especially reminded of Richards' depiction of this equilibrium in *Principles,* where he notes that "this balanced poise, stable through its power of inclusion, not through the force of its exclusions . . . is a general characteristic of all the most valuable experiences of the arts" (p. 248). Nonetheless, the shift from talk about inclusion of impulses to talk about inclusion of meanings represents an important clarification of the earlier statements. We saw earlier how, in accordance with the revised context theory, the *exclusion* of some of the different meanings of a word was managed by a determination of the framework of the utterance. Here, however, in the description of imaginative reading, Richards stresses the *inclusion* of these different meanings. In *Rhetoric,* Richards again emphasizes inclusion: the context theory of meaning discourages "our habit of behaving as though, if a passage means one thing it cannot at the same time mean another and an incompatible thing" (p. 38). In *Interpretation in Teaching* he notes that one phrase can mean fifty different and distinguishable things at one time (p. 10). In these passages Richards may be referring simply to the *possible* meanings suggested by a passage or phrase before it is interpreted, but that he probably has meaning by inclusion in mind is evidenced by his defense of the statement from *Rhetoric* in the preface to *Interpretation in Teaching:* he claims that he does not in this statement deny the principle of contradiction because "the principle of contradiction has to do with *logical* relations between meanings, not with the *psychological* concomitance of contradictory meanings" (p. vii). Multiple meaning, or ambiguity, is thus viewed in these passages not as something to be eliminated in interpreting a poetic utterance, but as central to that utterance. It is, for example, the "superfluity" of meaning of Keats' "Ode on a Grecian Urn," Richards notes in *Mencius,* which provides the suasive force of the poem (p. 117).

The second feature which distinguishes poetic utterance from non-poetic utterance, its untranslatability, is closely related to this superfluity of meaning. At several places in his later writings Richards expands the theme stressed in Chapter IX of *Coleridge,* that it is impossible to distill a "what" from a "how" in analyzing poetry, to reduce the poem to a message. We see it in the quotation from "The Future of Poetry" which heads this chapter. In this essay he labels the view that the what and the how are separable in poetry—that is, the view that the poet transmits a message by means of the poem—the "Vulgar Packaging View" *(Screens,* p. 124). Using Richards' notion of the fact of mind from *Coleridge* and his distinction of logical and psychological contradiction in the quotation cited above from *Interpretation in Teaching,* I would relate the untranslatability of an utterance and the superfluity of its meanings in this way: regarded as the presentation of a position, as something said, an utterance in which all the different meanings of its words were included would very likely be completely unintelligible. Such an utterance might be rendered intelligible, however, if we were to approach it instead from the standpoint of the utterer, as the *saying* of something. The resultant "psychological contradictions" might then reflect the divergent frameworks underlying the utterance and thus the divergent purposes supporting those frameworks. Such purposes could quite intelligibly coexist in the speaker. This different perspective is familiar to us from the distinction of doctrine and fact of mind in *Coleridge*. That distinction is enriched, however, by viewing it in terms of the context theory of meaning. Each meaning found to be relevant indirectly reflects a purpose governing the entire utterance. Thus the multiplicity of meanings reflects a multiplicity of purposes.

Poetic utterance is untranslatable, then, because its importance does not lie in what it says, but in the active discovery and balancing of the divergent purposes which control what it says. Richards repeatedly stresses the activity of the reader in the reading of poetry. In an early critical work, he suggests that the character Stavrogin in Dostoievsky's *The Possessed* is himself a work of art because he provides the opportunity for self-realization through the exercise of the reader's imagination.[28] In "The Interactions of Words" he says of a poem by Donne:

> There is a prodigious activity between the words as we read them. Following, exploring, realizing, *becoming* that activity is, I suggest, the essential thing in reading the poem. Understanding it is not a preparation for reading the poem. It is itself the poem. And it is a constructive, hazardous, free creative process, a process of conception through which a new being is growing in the mind. . . . We seem to create Donne's poem.[29]

28. "God of Dostoievsky," *Forum, 78* (1927), 96.
29. *Language of Poetry,* ed. Tate, p. 76.

In "Poetry as an Instrument of Research" he notes that "a poetic concern with the interactions of words" shifts our attention away from what is said to the process of saying *(Speculative Instruments,* p. 152). And, of course, there is the stress on the reader's activity in *Coleridge:* poetry provides a return to the fact of mind; with modern, difficult poetry, the poem is the "movements of exploration" involved in grasping it. A corollary of the poem's untranslatability is the *growth* in its meanings which Richards so often notes. Often poetry "utters not one meaning but a *movement* among meanings."[30] With imaginative passages, "we are invited to stretch our minds, and no one can flatter himself that he has ever finished the process of understanding such things."[31] The poem takes on more and more meanings as we attempt to balance its diverse purposes.

In addition to multiple meanings and untranslatability, a third feature of poetic language is completeness. The most fully developed account of the breadth of poetic utterance may be found in *Principles.* In its ability to accommodate opposed impulses, great art such as "tragedy is perhaps the most general, all-accepting, all-ordering experience known. It can take anything into its organisation, modifying it so that it finds a place. It is invulnerable . . ." to ironic treatment (p. 247). This inclusiveness stems directly from the untranslatability of poetry. Making no claim to be a statement, but merely acting as a focus of saying, the poem welcomes and indeed flourishes on antithetical interpretation.

The foregoing analysis of poetic discourse uncovers some of the sources of Richards' confusion of the peculiar fluid language of poetry with fluid assertive language. First, there is

30. *Rhetoric,* p. 48.
31. *Coleridge,* pp. 93–94.

the fact that both sorts of fluid discourse demand active interpretation. Second, poetic interpretation includes and rests upon active interpretation of assertive language. The choice of meanings of words depends upon the projection and testing of possible frameworks. Multiple meanings imply multiple interpretations, each requiring discovery of an underlying framework. Another source of confusion is the value of ambiguity in both assertive language and poetry. In *The Meaning of Meaning,* Richards sees multiple meanings primarily as traps for the unwary, as obstacles to be overcome in any attempt at clear communication. In later works such as "Multiple Definition," *Rhetoric,* and *How To Read a Page,* he stresses the values as much as the dangers of ambiguity. Not only would the attempt to replace the ranges of different meanings by different words be extremely wasteful, but "language, losing its subtlety with its suppleness, would lose also its power to serve us."[32] In part this praise stems from Richards' discovery of diverse frameworks in these multiple meanings, in part from his conviction that language affords the speaker a subtle opportunity to support such frameworks. When, however, Richards goes on to claim in *Rhetoric* that "ambiguity . . . [is] an inevitable consequence of the powers of language and . . . the indispensable means of most of our most important utterances—especially in Poetry and Religion" (p. 40), he seems to have in mind not these values of the ambiguity in assertive utterance, but the special value of ambiguity in poetic utterance.

The intrinsic value of reading poetry is implicit in Richards' analysis of poetic language. Throughout his writings he stresses the growth arising from reading poetry. It is evident in the self-realization in synaesthesis and the exemplary health cited in the quotations at the beginning of this chapter. It may be

32. *Rhetoric,* p. 73.

found throughout the early works, for example, in the "permanent modifications in the structure of the mind" which art brings about, in the righting of disturbed interests which leads to the balance of impulses, and in the stirring up of our habitual responses to effect a control over our feelings.[33] In the later works Richards cites the self-realizing growth in the imaginative experience, refers to the work of the poet as the "maintenance and enlargement of the human spirit through . . . molding and remolding the ever-varying flux," and claims that we read great writings "to stretch our minds."[34]

The growth he so often stresses is a growth in self-knowledge. If we view man as Richards does, as a creature who is "always pursuing his purposes; whatever he does is purposive in some degree,"[35] we see how reading poetry leads to this growth. The reader of poetry is absorbed in balancing the aims and purposes which underlie the frameworks he uncovers in reading. This process forces him to question his deepest nature, and thus to know himself more fully. The balance of impulses of Richards' earliest works and the exercise in choice of the latest share this value with the balances of interests and the balances in fluxes of the middle books. This is the value stemming from the superfluity, untranslatability, and completeness of the poetic utterance. It is the same value that Richards discovers in Coleridge's wind harp: "As the intellectual breeze plays on the organic harp, the music which arises orders all perception. It orders therefore the harp and the breeze as well."[36]

33. *Principles*, p. 132; *Science and Poetry*, p. 27; *Practical Criticism*, p. 239.

34. *Coleridge*, p. 69; "Interactions of Words," *Language of Poetry*, ed. Tate, p. 71; *How To Read a Page*, p. 15.

35. *How To Read a Page*, p. 227.

36. "Introduction," *The Portable Coleridge*, p. 39.

The wind harp provides the focus for Richards' most fully developed example of a reading of a poem, that of Coleridge's "Dejection," in *Coleridge on Imagination.*

> We cannot say, if we take the poem as a whole, that it contains the one doctrine [realist] rather than the other [projective]. The colours of Nature are a suffusion from the light of the mind, but the light of the mind in its turn, the shaping spirit of Imagination, comes from the mind's response to Nature:
>
>> To thee do all things live from pole to pole
>> Their life the eddying of thy living soul.
>
> *Eddying* is one of Coleridge's greatest imaginative triumphs. An eddy is in something, and is a conspicuous example of a balance of forces.
>
> This ambiguity (or rather, completeness) in Coleridge's thought here and his peculiar use of the Wind-Harp image, give us a concrete example of that self-knowledge, which . . . was . . . the principle of all his thinking.[37]

Ambiguity, untranslatability, and completeness characterize this poem. To conclude my description of Richards' views on poetic language, however, it will be more useful to turn from this concrete example to his discussions of a specific sort of emotive language, the metaphor.

Richards' changing treatment of metaphor in many ways reflects the growth of his more adequate account of emotive language. In addition to the "symbolic," or "prosaic," use of metaphor described in *The Meaning of Meaning,* as the "use

37. *Coleridge,* p. 152.

of one reference to a group of things between which a given relation holds, for the purpose of facilitating the discrimination of an analogous relation in another group" (p. 343), Richards distinguishes two sorts of "emotive" metaphor in his early works. One, described in *Practical Criticism,* is founded on the similarity between the feelings aroused by the objects referred to by the terms of the metaphor (pp. 221–22). The other, described in *The Meaning of Meaning,* is identified by its effects on the attitudes of the reader, such as those achieved by the "contrast, conflict, harmony, interinanimation, and equilibrium" of the terms of the metaphor (p. 378). In *Principles* he adds the effect achieved by the variety which metaphor introduces into a poem (p. 240). These two uses recall the first two characterizations of emotive language, which we found to be inadequate: emotive language as language used non-referentially and emotive language as language used to arouse attitudes.

In keeping with his third conception of the nature of emotive language, Richards combines elements of the earlier two analyses of metaphor in the later accounts of *The Philosophy of Rhetoric* and *Interpretation in Teaching.* In *Rhetoric* he introduces the terms "tenor" and "vehicle" to distinguish the elements of a metaphor. In "A man is a wolf," for example, "man" is the tenor and "wolf" the vehicle. He notes that it is the similarity between the tenor and the vehicle which constitutes the ground of all metaphors (chs. 5–6), but he adds:

> In general, there are very few metaphors in which disparities between tenor and vehicle are not as much operative as the similarities. . . . The peculiar modification of the tenor which the vehicle brings about is even more the work of their unlikenesses than of their likenesses. (p.127)

Richards here describes the collocation of terms in metaphor as leading to a sort of intercourse, transaction, or transference between their associated contexts. In metaphor we come to respond to one thing in terms of our responses to another. In so doing, however, we do not abandon our original responses. He illustrates the point in a discussion of the relationship between mind and river in Denham's lines on the Thames:

> O could I flow like thee, and make thy stream
> My great exemplar as it is my theme!
> Though deep, yet clear; though gentle, yet not dull;
> Strong without rage; without o'erflowing, full.

Richards comments: "The more carefully and attentively we go over the senses and implications of *deep, clear, gentle, strong* and *full* as they apply to a stream and to a mind, the less shall we find the resemblances between vehicle and tenor counting and the more will the vehicle, the river, come to seem an excuse for saying about the mind something which could not be said about the river." For instance, it is "deep" in the sense of "mysterious" and "rich in knowledge and power." Nevertheless, "the river is not a mere excuse, or a decoration only, a gilding of the moral pill. The vehicle is still controlling the mode in which the tenor forms" (p. 122).

The metaphoric relationship between mind and river forces us to concentrate on the variety of interpretations that we afford to the mind. Thus the metaphor does not *say* anything directly about the mind, but merely provides the occasion for multiple sayings. Metaphors differ, Richards remarks in both *Rhetoric* (pp. 100–01) and *Interpretation in Teaching* (pp. 121–22), as to whether greater emphasis is placed on the tenor or on the vehicle, or equal emphasis placed on each. The importance of the comparison, however, never lies simply in the respect in which the two items are the same. It is undoubtedly because the meaning of metaphor lies in the movements involved in its interpretation that Richards stresses its untranslatability and remarks that metaphor reflects a completion and a development of sensation, and not a mere substitute for it.[38]

Richards' discussion of metaphor in *Rhetoric* not only illustrates his most adequate analysis of emotive language but also provides us with another example of his confusion of the interpretation of poetic with assertive utterances. Metaphor, he claims in Chapter V, is not an unusual feature of language, but is really its usual feature. In fact, every word is a metaphor: "A word is normally a substitute for (or means) not one discrete past impression but a combination of general aspects. Now that is itself a summary account of the principle of metaphor" (p. 93). In part, Richards is merely trying to emphasize the importance of his discussion of metaphor by this claim that all words are metaphors. But this assertion also represents a confusion of the need for flexibility and intelligence in all interpretation with the special characteristics of the interpretation of poetic language. His calling all words "metaphors" is grounded in the context theory of meaning. A word is a nexus on which are focused its various uses in similar situations in the past. The strength of metaphor, we have seen, derives from its forcing us to see two or more meanings of a word as relevant to its interpretation. But the mere fact that a word can mean different things, and has meant different things under differing circumstances in the past, does not mean that its force always depends upon the relevance of several of these different meanings in the present situation. Indeed, all words, through the context theory of meaning, are *potentially* metaphors in that they allow of diverse uses. Only under

38. *Rhetoric,* pp. 128–31; *Interpretation in Teaching,* ch. 8.

special circumstances, however, is this metaphoric quality released.

Metaphor is not the only example of emotive language, but it is a clear one. Perhaps it is for this reason that in his recent discussions of the nature of emotive language, Richards has stressed the importance of the study of metaphor. In "Emotive Meaning Again"[39] he justifies such study by noting that, although metaphor is sometimes used referentially, "field investigations into how people interpret metaphor become hard to distinguish from inquiry into their responses to emotive language" (*Speculative Instruments,* p. 48). Some of the questions he envisages as arising in a study of metaphor—for example, "What sorts or orders of ?truth? are appropriate to (or possible to) whatever may be ?said? only through metaphor? When and how is what is ?said? through metaphor the same as what is said without it?" (p. 46)—clearly indicate the now familiar differences between emotive and referential language.

The activity of reading poetry, according to this third characterization of emotive language, thus engages the individual in a markedly different way than does his reading of assertive language. Observable differences in the two activities—the growth of meaning in the poetic experience, the untranslatability of poetic discourse, and the completeness of the experience—are merely the surface manifestations of the peculiarly important value of poetry, the involvement with purposes which stems from a concern with the saying of the poem rather than with what is said by it. Criticism of this complex account must await the tracing of its implications through Richards' views on the approach to poetry, criticism, and the outcome of reading poetry, its instrumental value.

39. *Speculative Instruments,* pp. 39–56.

I might note in concluding this chapter how the analysis herein is more satisfactory than the other two Richardsian analyses of emotive language. It is similar to the first in empha-sizing the *expressing* of feelings and attitudes and to the second in stressing the value of *balancing* such feelings and attitudes. But whereas both of the other views were incomplete and vague, this third view combines them while apparently avoid-ing ambiguity and pictorial appeals. The discussion of fluid language also fills in central gaps in the theory sketched in *Coleridge*. It clarifies Richards' account of imagination by relating his analyses of such items as the coadunation of mean-ings in imaginative poetry and the growth and self-realization of the imaginative experience. Furthermore, it relates his de-scription of imagination with other topics in *Coleridge*. We can now appreciate the claim Richards makes for the greater mythologies:

> Through such mythologies our will is collected, our pow-ers unified, our growth controlled. Through them the in-finitely divergent strayings of our being are brought into "balance or reconciliation." . . . Without his mythologies man is only a cruel animal without a soul . . .—he is a congeries of possibilities without order and without aim. (pp. 171–72)

We understand more fully his discussion of the "best poetry," the poetry whose being consists in the journey itself and not in any end reached. It is valuable because it absorbs the reader in purposes and choices, and not because it presents him with any single directive. A study of Richards' other writings has thus clarified some of the hints we found in *Coleridge* con-cerning the activity of reading poetry. Let us see what these other works tell us about the proper approach to the poem.

4

The Approach to the Poem: Poetry and Criticism

It has to be recognised that all our natural turns of speech are misleading, especially those we use in discussing works of art. We become so accustomed to them that even when we are aware that they are ellipses, it is easy to forget the fact. . . . We continually talk as though things possess qualities, when what we ought to say is that they cause effects in us of one kind or another [—] the fallacy of "projecting" the effect and making it a quality of its cause. . . . Such terms as . . . "rhythm," "stress," "plot," "character" . . . are instances. All these terms are currently used as though they stood for qualities inherent in things outside the mind. . . . Even the difficulty of discovering, in the case of poetry, what thing other than print and paper is there for these alleged qualities to belong to, has not checked the tendency. . . . We are forced to speak as though certain physical objects— . . . marks printed on paper, . . . are what we are talking about. And yet the remarks we make as critics do not apply to such objects but to states of mind, to experiences.

We must be prepared then to translate, into phrases pedantic and uncouth, all the too simple utterances which the conversational decencies exact.[1]

As we swing over from an attitude to words as signs to an attitude to them as *containing in themselves* a part or whole of the meaning we give to them, we get quite another sense for *word*. . . . To say that a word is or contains in itself its meaning will seem only a short (and sometimes convenient) way of saying that it is a sign with a certain meaning appropriated to it. But, if we are not explicitly asking ourselves questions about how we read, but just discussing literary matters, we do, on innumerable occasions, not only *talk* but actually think as though the words and their meanings are one and the same.

Anyone who doubts this may consider the parallel case of *poem*. How often, when we discuss a poem, do we *not* include a meaning as well as the marks on the paper, in our acting definition? A meaning is always what we are talking about, never the signs. What we say about the poem is true (if it is) only about the meaning. It is inapplicable, in fact nonsense, as a commentary on the signs. And this is not a matter of ellipsis, of our laziness and disinclination to make elaborate analytic statements. This investment of the words with a meaning is an essential part of the right reading of them.[2]

Nothing has contributed more to the ordinary critic's view that the late Richards repudiated the early Richards than the

1. *Principles,* pp. 20–22.
2. *Coleridge,* pp. 106–07.

apparent about-face represented in these two passages. What is called a "fallacy" in the earlier passage is cited as "essential to right reading" in the second. The "ellipses" which need to be translated "into phrases pedantic and uncouth" of the first passage are "not . . . matter[s] of ellipsis" in the second. One can try to minimize the apparent change: Richards' statement in the second passage—that we always talk about the meaning of a poem, never its signs—may seem close to his earlier assertion that certain words never refer to physical objects but always to states of mind. But his insistence in the later passage that the words of the poem are invested with their meanings undercuts this similarity of statement. One had better try to explain the change, not explain it away.

I have contended thus far that Richards never really changed his fundamental ideas drastically; he merely found less misleading (if vaguer) modes of presenting them. Our question concerning these passages, then, should be: What is the misleading framework underlying the early statement that Richards avoids in the later statement? Before embarking on a detailed analysis of the two passages in an attempt to answer this question, I should explain why I think that an illumination of Richards' discussion of projection will provide us with insights into his views on the criticism of poetry. Richards, we saw in *Coleridge,* is guilty, as are most aestheticians, of confusing the special concerns of the aesthetician with those of the critic or reader. Occasionally, however, he does distinguish these concerns, and the second passage above would seem to be a case in point. Projection of meaning is appropriate "if we are not explicitly asking ourselves questions about how we read, but just discussing literary matters." However silly projection may seem to the aesthetician as a description of the nature of the poem, it is just the attitude required by the reader or critic. Perhaps the trouble with the anti-projective position of the first passage is that it does not clearly provide answers to either party's concerns.

An investigation of the critical theory developed in the early works (the first passage at the head of this chapter is from *Principles of Literary Criticism*) indicates the shortcomings of the anti-projective position. This investigation does not lead, as did my study of the first two senses of "emotive language" in the preceding chapter, to incomplete characterizations. Instead, we find that the scheme is too rich—indeed, that it is incurably ambiguous. We can best grasp this ambiguity, which is centered in Richards' use of the expression "poetic experience," by considering his "communicative" theory of poetry.

In *Principles,* Richards defines a poem as a "class of experiences which do not differ in any character more than a certain amount . . . from a standard experience" (pp. 226–27). He defines the standard experience both as the experience which led the poet to write what he did and as the "relevant" experience of the poet when contemplating his own completed composition. Thus, "Westminster Bridge" is not a series of words on paper, it is a class of experiences somewhat similar to an experience Wordsworth once had (or might have had). Only the reader who has a similar experience can fairly evaluate the poem, for he alone can be said truly to have "read" the poem and not "misread" it (p. 227). This definition of a poem, which so clearly provides the basis for the anti-projective account above, is grounded in Richards' conviction that the only adequate way to view poetry is as a *communication* between poet and reader. Thus he says, in *The Foundations of Aesthetics:* "It is odd that Mr. Fry . . . attaches so much importance to Tolstoi's least original tenet. That art is the *communication* of

something may be regarded as common ground to all aesthetics
. . ." (p. 61n.). And in *Principles* he says that "the arts are the
supreme form of the communicative activity" (p. 26).

Richards relies heavily upon Tolstoy's theory of communication in developing his own in *Principles,* and there are many
similarities between the two. In *What Is Art?*[3] Tolstoy characterizes art as the communication of emotion or feeling. It is
not merely the presentation of a feeling for the scrutiny of the
perceiver, but rather the actual *infection* of the perceiver with
the same feeling that the artist has experienced. To infect the
perceiver the artist must be sincere, that is, he must really have
experienced the feeling and it must be "evoked" in him at the
time of composition (pp. 120–23, 183, 186, 193, 229). The
evoked feeling controls the course of its "embodiment" in the
external medium. Filled with the feeling, and blessed with an
elementary school background in the principles of art, the artist
will compose or paint or write so that his own experience will
be aroused in the spectator. In the handling of his materials he
will capture the "wee bit" which marks the difference between
genuine and counterfeit art (pp. 200–01, 269–70). An obvious
difference between Richards' communicative scheme and Tolstoy's lies in the nature of what is communicated from artist to
receiver. For Tolstoy's emotions and feelings Richards substi-
tutes "experiences." But, as we shall see below, the ambiguity in
Richards' use of the word "experience" blurs the difference
and exposes Richards' theory to some serious shortcomings
of Tolstoy's.

The outrageous critical pronouncements of Tolstoy's *What
Is Art?* have been frequently criticized. In *Principles,* Richards
himself stresses the crankiness of Tolstoy's views:

3. Trans. Alymer Maude (London, 1955; first app. 1898).

> With magnificent defiance of accepted values, and the
> hardness of heart of a supreme doctrinaire, one after
> another of the unassailables is toppled from its eminence.
> Shakespeare, Dante, Goethe, etc., are rejected; Wagner
> in especial is the object of a critical *tour de force*. In
> their place are set *A Tale of Two Cities, The Chimes,
> Adam Bede, Les Miserables* . . . and *Uncle Tom's Cabin.*
> All art which does not directly urge the union of men, or
> whose appeal is suspected to be limited to cultured and
> aristocratic circles, is condemned. (pp. 65–66)

Richards indicates here only one of the reasons for Tolstoy's
strange opinions. It is certainly true that sentimental egali-
tarianism supports his rejection of accepted masterpieces.
Nonetheless, the communicative framework itself is a second
important factor in this rejection. One of the most noteworthy
features of *What Is Art?* is its emphasis on the passivity of the
person appreciating art. This is most explicitly stated in Tolstoy's formal definition of the work of art:

> If a man *without exercising effort and without altering his
> standpoint,* on reading, hearing, or seeing another man's
> work experiences a mental condition which unites him
> with that man and with others who are also affected by
> that work, then the object evoking that condition is a
> work of art. (p. 227, my italics)

The same point—that the appreciation of true art is spon-
taneous and immediate—is stressed throughout the book. One
need not work at understanding art; if such work is necessary,
it is clear that the piece is not genuine (pp. 176–80). All responsibility for adequate communication lies with the artist.
He must be sincere in order to get the wee bit right. The

trouble with Shakespeare and Bach (a trouble they share with the French Symbolists) is that they are insincere, and their works are consequently too obscure (ch. 10, pp. 248–49). Difficult art is like music which has not simply melody, but harmony as well: it takes special training to grasp (p. 245). The Vogul play and the peasants' singing share an infectious simplicity which is absent from *Hamlet* and Beethoven's Opus 101 (ch. 14).

Tolstoy's praise of the simple and rejection of the difficult in art result, in part, from his description of art as an infection of receiver by artist. Anyone who adopts a communicative framework has to explain how distortion of communication is prevented. The obvious points at which distortion may occur are in the embodiment of the artist's experience in the vehicle and in the recovery of the experience from the vehicle by the interpreter. There is also the problem of distortion of the vehicle, but this is less serious in literature than in the other arts. Tolstoy has solved the problem of distortion by placing all responsibility for successful communication of the experience on the sincere artist, whose art is not "true" unless he provides an obvious embodiment, thus eliminating the possibility of distortion by the perceiver. The resulting account, however mysterious it may be (he never explains, for instance, why or how sincerity plus elementary technical skill assure effectiveness), clearly fulfills the demands of the communicative framework.

Richards, of course, does not share Tolstoy's penchant for simple art. Were the communicative framework to necessitate the exclusion of difficult art, Richards would never have adopted it. However, by concentrating on the other end of the communicative process, by placing strict controls on the *reading* of poetry so that the onus of successful communication lies more on the reader than the poet, he is able both to use the framework and to preserve his estimate of the worth of difficult literature. This does not mean that Richards completely ignores the embodiment phase of communication; still, his treatment of the poet and his creative activities is little more than perfunctory. He simply adopts Tolstoy's claim that sincerity effects communication: when the poet truly feels the experience he is trying to communicate, he communicates it successfully.[4]

Richards' task is to show how the reader, in confronting the poetic vehicle, undergoes an experience similar to the experience which the poet embodied in it. This experience typically consists of a balanced set of impulses, for the poet, because of his sensitivity, has been simultaneously affected by a large number of diverse stimuli.[5] In *The Foundations of Aesthetics,* Richards pictures the confrontation which leads to the "aesthetic" emotion:

> It is plain that a description of what happens when we feel aesthetic emotion . . . would fall into two halves. There would be a long psychological story about the organization of our impulses and instincts and of the special momentary setting of them due to our environment and our immediate past history on the one hand. On the other a physico-physiological account of the work of art as a stimulus, describing also its immediate sensory effects, and the impulses which these bring into play. The responsibility for the aesthetic emotion which results must be shared among all these factors. Even if we can detect some of the more important factors in the psychological conditions and group them as constant, as we seem to do when we talk of "sensitive persons," we are still left with a very complicated set of conditions. (p. 63)

4. See *Principles,* chs. 4, 23; also *Science and Poetry,* ch. 4.
5. *Principles,* ch. 22.

Richards had a choice of two ways of explaining how this confrontation yields a set of attitudes. Impulses, we saw in Chapter 3, may be distorted to yield attitudes either through interference with impulses currently characterizing the interpreter, or through complex interaction with other impulses aroused in the experience. It is not surprising to discover that Richards relies mainly upon the latter explanation to account for the way in which attitudes arise in the reading of poetry. The communicative framework requires that the set of attitudes (which constitutes the heart of the poetic experience)[6] be not only the culmination of a *particular* reader's confrontation with the poem, but also the culmination of *all* qualified readers' confrontations with the poem. Or, to be more precise, all qualified readers must share experiences "which do not differ within certain limits from . . . [the poet's] experience."[7] The similarity of experiences could be accounted for by the claim that, when combined with the impulses stimulated by the poem, different internal configurations of different readers produce similar attitudes in each reader. But this unlikely transformation seems much less plausible than the similarity which would result if the internal impulses of each reader were neutralized during reading, and the complexities of the vehicle were allowed to produce the attitudes. The second explanation seems even more feasible when we realize that it not only accounts for the development of attitudes in the experience, but also supplies a test for the competence of any reader of the poem. A "sensitive person" becomes one who can properly *neutralize* his internal condition while reading.

To some extent this neutralization can be accounted for by characteristics of the vehicle itself. Richards finds that the

6. Ibid., p. 132.
7. Ibid., p. 226.

formal features—rhythm and rhyme—manage through their uniformity to control the reader's response and to keep it free from irrelevant memories, and through their primitiveness to free the reader from his customary inhibitions and ordinary responses.[8] Unless Richards were willing to call all difficult poetry "counterfeit," however, the vehicle could not always be counted upon to provide the requisite neutralization. Just as vital is the reader's *approach* to the poem. Richards' most extensive account of the approach which the reader should adopt to the poem may be found in his discussions in *Practical Criticism* of the ten sorts of difficulties which most frequently trouble readers: difficulties in construing (making out the meaning of) the poem; difficulties in sensuous apprehension; difficulties connected with the place of imagery in poetic reading; mnemonic irrelevancies; stock responses; sentimentality; inhibition; doctrinal adhesions; technical presuppositions; and critical presuppositions.[9] To avoid these pitfalls the reader should have the "special communicative gifts" which Richards mentions in *Principles:* "discrimination, suggestibility, free and clear resuscitation of elements of past experience *disentangled from one another,* and control of irrelevant personal details and accidents" (p. 180). Discrimination enables the reader to distinguish clearly the different ways in which language is being used in the poem and makes him awake to every nuance of rhythm and rhyme. Suggestibility prevents inappropriate presuppositions concerning imagery, technique, and value. Resuscitation of elements of past experience guards against response in terms of stock responses—which are the result, Richards explains, of a removal from experience—as well as against inappropriate sentimental or inhibitory responses. Control of irrelevant personal details eliminates mnemonic ir-

8. Ibid., pp. 192–93; 244–45.
9. *Practical Criticism*, pp. 13–17.

relevancies and unwarranted doctrinal adhesions. In general, the necessary approach is one which is unusually susceptible to every feature of the work because all distracting personal factors have been eliminated. In the early works, the exclusion of personal factors is often related to communicative needs.

> In the arts . . . severance from . . . personal particular circumstances [particular passions, needs, desires or circumstances of the hearer] is necessary for the sake of universality. . . .[10]

> The characteristics by which aesthetic experience is usually defined—. . . impersonality, disinterestedness and detachment . . .—are really two sets of quite different characters. One set [is] . . . merely conditions of communication. . . . [11] [The other set Richards characterizes as the outcome of the synaesthetic experience.]

> [The poem] differs from many other experiences . . . in . . . [its] communicability. For these reasons when we experience it, or attempt to, we must preserve it from contamination, from the irruptions of personal particularities. We must keep the poem undisturbed by these or we fail to read it and have some other experience instead. For these reasons we establish a severance, we draw a boundary between the poem and what is not the poem in our experience.[12]

Richards' scheme seems initially very different from Tolstoy's in its stress on the reader's active part in successful

---

10. *Meaning of Meaning,* pp. 378–79.
11. *Principles,* pp. 248–49.
12. Ibid., p. 78.

artistic communication. A careful study of this activity indicates, however, that it is directed largely to the negative goal of freeing the reader from irrelevant distractions so that the poem may work effectively upon him. In a sense, then, the passivity of Tolstóy's theory is preserved. The point may be seen in this statement appearing toward the end of *Practical Criticism:* "All that arguments or principles can do is to protect us from irrelevancies, red-herrings and disturbing preconceptions. . . . They may preserve us from bad arguments but they cannot supply good ones" (pp. 302–03). Richards here has in mind "arguments and principles" concerning the value of the poem as well as its meaning. We shall see shortly why such arguments or principles may not be used directly or positively in an evaluation of the work, why "no theory, no description, of poetry can be trusted which is not too intricate to be applied" (p. 302). Here I want to point out that the statement also indicates the largely negative function of those arguments or principles needed to help fulfill the communicative process, to help the reader achieve the "experience" of the poem. In affording the reader a more direct contact with the poem by freeing him from personal distractions, such critical principles assume the status of what Richards later calls "policeman doctrines." These are doctrines, such as the context theory of meaning, which "are designed on the model of an ideal police-force, not to make any of us do anything but to prevent other people from interfering unduly with our lawful activities.[13] In "The Future of Poetry" *(Screens,* p. 120) Richards, applying the language of the communications engineer to poetic communication, depicts the "many ways in which Reception can go wrong" as "noise," and offers as typical examples "hasty assumptions as to meter" and the "whole circus of technical and critical preconceptions" described in *Practical Criticism.*

13. *Rhetoric,* p. 38.

There is no reason to complain about Richards' insistence on the need for excluding irrelevant personal factors from the reading of a poem. What is unfortunate is that in so depicting the reader's activity, he seems to forget about that involvement with purposes which we saw in the last chapter to be central to his account of the activity of reading poetry. Actually, he never explicitly excludes such involvement in his earlier discussions of the reader's activity; rather, he equivocates. Thus, he states in *Practical Criticism:*

> That the one and only goal of all critical endeavours, of all interpretation, appreciation, exhortation, praise or abuse, is improvement in communication may seem an exaggeration. But in practice it is so. The whole apparatus of critical rules and principles is a means to the attainment of finer, more precise, more discriminating communication. There is, it is true, a valuation side to criticism. When we have solved, completely, the communication problem, when we have got, perfectly, the experience, *the mental condition* relevant to the poem, we have still to judge it, still to decide upon its worth. But the later question nearly always settles itself; or rather, our inmost nature and the nature of the world in which we live decide it for us. Our prime endeavour must be to get the relevant mental condition and then see what happens. (p. 11)

Precisely what is this "experience," this "mental condition relevant to the poem"? Is it a balanced set of impulses received from passive submission to the vehicle? Or is it rather the active *balancing* of purposes discovered in the free and fluid reading of the work?

Richards' analysis of the language of poetry which I developed in Chapter 2 certainly calls for the latter interpretation. So also, interestingly, does his account in *Practical Criticism* of the *evaluation* of poetry which, acccording to the statement just quoted, represents the "other side" of communication. Evaluation of a poem is accomplished, Richards claims, by the choice of the individual:

> In these moments of sheer decision . . . the mind becomes most plastic, and selects, at the incessant multiple shifting cross-roads, the direction of its future development.
>
> The critical act is the starting-point, not the conclusion, of an argument. The personality stands balanced between the particular experience which is the realized poem and the whole fabric of its past experiences and developed habits of mind.

Behind the decision is the strain of a largely unconscious struggle:

> But when the conflict resolves itself, . . . the mind clears, and new energy wells up; after the pause a collectedness supervenes; behind our rejection or acceptance (even of a minor poem) we feel the sanction and authority of the self-completing spirit.

Richards stresses the activity underlying choice:

> Mere acquiescent immersion in good poetry can give us, of course, much that is valuable. Acquiescent immersion in bad poetry entails a corresponding penalty. But the greater values can only be gained by making poetry the occasion for those momentous decisions of the will. (pp. 303–05)

In Part Four of *Practical Criticism,* Richards defends the subjectivity implicit in this account of evaluation:

> When our interests are developing in opposed directions we cannot agree in our ultimate valuations and choices. Unless we are to become most undesirably standardised, differences of opinion about poetry must continue. . . . [These different opinions may belie persons in different stages of moral development, but it is still] less important to like "good" poetry and dislike "bad," than to be able to use them both as a means of ordering our minds. . . . Most of our responses are not real, are not our own, and this is just the difficulty. (pp. 347–49)

The tone of these passages anticipates that of Richards' later works. But the themes, as well, are familiar from *Coleridge on Imagination.* The "self-completing spirit" recalls the self-growth and realization accomplished in imagination; the freedom of the choice echoes the freedom underlying the realizing intuition and the recognizing of imaginative poetry through freedom. One is reminded of his characterization of judgment in *Coleridge* as an "act of living," a "choice."

My investigations in Chapter 3 can, then, be of use in understanding these analyses of evaluation. I suggest that Richards is thinking along the following lines: when we are involved in knowing or realizing ourselves most fully we are absorbed in the interplay of the divergent purposes which underlie our existence as human beings. Our choice of a poem determines "the directions of the mind's future development" in that reading it affords us a model for the balancing of our interests. The poem does not merely offer us an aim or purpose, or even a balanced set of impulses. Such may be the result of "acquiescent immersion" in good poetry, but this merely provides us with the

103

"conclusion," not the "starting-point" of an argument. Only when seen as an occasion for actively balancing purposes is the poem able to provide the link between the mind's past experiences and habits and its future development. To meet our needs, to serve our interests, the poem cannot be passively absorbed; it must be actively recreated.

This theory of evaluation presents a host of problems, though some of them can be fairly easily handled. It may seem, for instance, that Richards is overstressing the content of the work and understressing its formal properties. Cannot the reader value a work highly for its technique, though thinking little of its message, or disvalue the work for its awkwardness, though accepting its message? Richards would undoubtedly demur: for him there is no distinction between a content and a form, a technique and a message. There is no *what* as distinct from a *how* in the complete utterance of poetry. There is only the entire, living utterance to be accepted or rejected for its success or failure in focusing needs.

While Richards' solution to this problem—whether we agree with it or not—is fairly evident in his writings, other difficulties raised by the theory of evaluation are not so easily overcome. There is, for instance, the tension between the subjectivism of this account and the objective appeal we frequently find elsewhere. There is also the confusion of considerations of evaluation and value in Richards' insistence that his "subjectivistic" account is really not very subjectivistic because individuals can be evaluated on an objective scale even though each of them will evaluate poems differently according to his immediate needs.[14] I shall try to deal with these difficulties in my sixth chapter. But this glance at Richards' views on evaluation does point to an interpretation of the "mental condition"

14. *Practical Criticism,* p. 348. See also *Principles* (3rd ed. New York, 1955; first publ. 1928), p. 288.

relevant to the poem, the "experience" of the poem which is the outcome of the interpretive process, as an active balancing of purposes, not as a received balance of impulses.

Although an interpretation of the "experience communicated by the poem" as being strongly dependent upon the activity of the reader is possible for the aesthetician, it is still unusual. Moreover, it is highly unlikely that one concerned with poetry from the standpoint of the reader or critic would hit upon such an interpretation, for what, in their view, is the focus of this active concern, the poetic vehicle, has been virtually dismissed from consideration. These facts explain why Richards de-emphasizes the communicative framework in his later works. It is supposed to provide the basis for an improved language of criticism and for a definition of a "correct reading,"[15] but it is ambiguous for the aesthetician and completely misleading to critics and readers. The characterization of poetry in Richards' later writings may, as we shall discover, do little toward clarifying its ontological status, but at least it provides an unambiguous account upon which a critical theory can be built. To emphasize the ambiguity underlying the communicative framework, we might look finally at Richards' recent attack, in the "Future of Poetry," on the "Vulgar Packaging View" which tries to separate a *what* from a *how* in entire utterances.

> According to this, here's the poet having a ¹poetic experience¹ poor fellow. (I should put shrieks of derision round every phrase of this account.) Then he wraps it up well in a neat and elegant verbal package—air, damp and rust, mould, moth and fungus proof, guaranteed to keep forever . . . and sells us it so! We unwrap it, if we can, and enjoy the contents. We have the ¹poetic experience¹, believe it or not! *(Screens,* p. 124)

15. *Principles,* chs. 3, 30.

The strange thing is that this representation of one of the "oldest errors," sounds a little like the early Richards himself—or, perhaps, like an obvious way of interpreting the early Richards. He had to alter his descriptions, if only to avoid such an interpretation.

In his later works Richards does not abandon his view that the poem is a communication between the poet and the reader. Indeed, in "The Interactions of Words" he cites the "correspondence *between*" minds along with the "maintenance of stability *within*" them as "the poetic problem,"[16] and uses a communication engineer's diagram to depict the poetic process in "The Future of Poetry." But in this late essay we find Richards stressing a new point, which prohibits what is communicated from being interpreted as an experience actively prepared for and passively received by the reader. Speaking first of his own essay, Richards notes: "How you understand me will depend upon what I go on to say but more still on what you find (now or later) to say to yourself (or to others) about it all" *(Screens,* p. 112). And later in the essay, more specifically in reference to the reception of poetry, Richards remarks that it is surprising that communication "is as good as sometimes it seems to be." But by success he here means "having *more or less the same potentialities*—not necessarily actualities—it had before its death into the signal" (p. 118). If reception leads "to an organism having potentialities comparable to those belonging to what was transmitted, the poem, we say, has then been *read* (as opposed to being *misread)"* (p. 119). The stress on *potentialities* communicated, not actualities, is an attempt to avoid the ambiguity underlying the earlier distinction he makes, in *Principles,* between having read or misread a poem in terms of the similarity of the reader's experience with that of the poet.

16. *Language of Poetry,* ed. Tate, p. 71.

What is communicated in "The Future of Poetry" is clearly not a balanced set of impulses. It is an opportunity, a set of potentialities, for self-growth.

Even more characteristic of Richards' later writings, however, is his tendency to play down the communicative aspect of poetry, and to replace the old communicative model of language with a new model in which language is viewed as having a life of its own, as embodying the vitality of the poet. By avoiding the ambiguity of the earlier representation, the new picture provides a sounder foundation for a critical theory. The best-known statement of the new view exists in *Rhetoric:*

> So far from verbal language being a "compromise for a language of intuition"—a thin, but better-than-nothing, substitute for real experience,—language, well used, is a *completion* and does what the intuitions of sensations by themselves cannot do. Words are the meeting points at which regions of experience which can never combine in sensation or intuition, come together. They are the occasion and the means of that growth which is the mind's endless endeavour to order itself. That is why we have language. It is no mere signalling system. It is the instrument of all our distinctively human development, of everything in which we go beyond the other animals.
>
> Thus, to present language as working only through the sensations it reinstates, is to turn the whole process upside down. It overlooks what is important in Mallarmé's *dictum* that the poet does not write with thoughts (or with ideas or sensations or beliefs or desires or feelings, we may add) but with words. (pp. 130–31)

This emphasis on the words of the poem leads to an expected de-emphasis of the poet and his experiences. In *Principles,* the arts are said to be of particular value because "they

107

spring from and perpetuate hours in the lives of exceptional people . . . " (p. 32). "We pass as a rule from a chaotic to a better organized state . . . typically through the influence of other minds. Literature and the arts are the chief means by which these influences are diffused."[17] Several years later, in *How To Read a Page,* he claims that

> the reader, as opposed to the biographer, is not concerned with what as historical fact was going on in the author's mind when he penned the sentence, but with what the words—given the rest of the language—may mean. We do not read Shakespeare, or Plato, or Lao Tzu, or Homer, or the Bible, to discover what their authors —about whom otherwise we know so little—were thinking. We read them for the sake of the things their words —if we understand them—can do for us. . . . Understanding them . . . is using them to stretch our minds as they have stretched the minds of so many different readers through the centuries. (pp. 14–15)

In his latest writings Richards even *contrasts* the poem with the poet's experience. He would like to alter Shelley's "Poets are the unacknowledged legislators of the world" to read " *'Poems* are the unacknowledged legisla*tion* of the world.' That would take the weight off the poor, brief, human, limited poet and put it on the august, enduring, superhuman artifice of eternity the poet can be the means of bringing into existence."[18] A poem, he claims in another late work, is greater than its author and has its meaning whether the author finds the meaning in it or not.[19]

17. *Principles* (3rd ed. New York, 1955; first publ. 1928), p. 57.
18. *Screens,* p. 106.
19. "Poetic Process and Literary Analysis," *Style in Language,* ed. Thomas A. Sebeok (Cambridge, Mass., 1960), pp. 12–13.

One device which Richards frequently adopts in his later works to point up the vitality of poetic language is to liken it to a living organism. In "Notes toward an Agreement between Literary Criticism and Some of the Sciences," Richards depicts the literary critic as complaining that "the Linguistic Scientist . . . does not know how to respect the language. He does not yet have a conception of the language which would make it respectable. He thinks of it as a *code* and has not yet learned that it is an organ—the supreme organ of the mind's self-ordering growth."[20] In more than one passage he follows Coleridge in likening language to a plant, and words to parts of the plant.[21] Though dependent to some extent on external circumstances, the life of poetic language, like the plant's, depends as much upon the complex interrelationship of its parts. Language is also seen as a society whose members operate in terms of a "code," that is, "a collection of regulations or agreements, or observances."[22] Richards entitles a recent paper "How Does a Poem Know When It Is Finished?" but explains that he has not committed the pathetic fallacy:

> My title doesn't attribute anything to poems that they do not fully have. They are living, feeling, knowing *beings* in their own right; the so-called metaphor that treats the poem as organic is not a metaphor, but a literal description. A poem is an activity, seeking to become itself.[23]

An obvious extension of these characterizations of the poem as a living organism would be to view it as a true surrogate for

20. *Speculative Instruments*, p. 9.
21. *Coleridge*, pp. 12, 52–53; *Rhetoric*, pp. 12, 110–12.
22. *Screens*, p. 115; see also *How To Read a Page*, p. 103.
23. "How Does a Poem Know When It Is Finished?" *Parts and Wholes*, ed. Daniel Lerner (New York, 1963), p. 165.

the poet, as a living person. Richards frequently hints at this move. He claims that "language . . . is the mind itself at work and these interactions of words are interdependencies of our own being."[24] He reduces understanding ourselves to understanding words.[25] But it is in *Rhetoric* that we find the most explicit relationship:

> Thus in happy living the same patterns are exemplified and the same risks of error are avoided as in tactful and discerning reading. The general form of the interpretative process is the same, with a small-scale instance—the right understanding of a figure of speech—or with a large-scale instance—the conduct of a friendship. (p. 136)

Richards' insistence on projection of meanings into the words of the poem follows directly from this emphasis on the vitality of the poetic vehicle. The poem should be viewed not as a set of dead marks, but as a set of living, interacting meanings. Unfortunately, the only place where Richards draws an explicit relation between these themes is in an extremely difficult passage from "The Future of Poetry." The poem (and each of its words) is a union of *"signifiant* and *signifié* (in Saussure's terms)"—Richards has previously distinguished the physical vehicle from its meaning—"a union in which the body, while it is alive, is not to be conceived apart from that which informs it, that which it embodies, and conversely" *(Screens,* p. 120). Richards goes on to state—in a passage whose meaning is rendered highly obscure by his free use of direct quotations from Wordsworth's *Prelude*—that the duality between the words and their meanings is "woven" by the

24. "Interactions of Words," *Language of Poetry,* ed. Tate, p. 73.
25. *How To Read a Page,* pp. 186–87.

"filial" bond between us and "this active universe." Richards could mean a number of things by this "poetic plaiting," but a part of his meaning would seem to be that the projection of the meanings of words into those words is an instance of our relationship with living things in the universe. We have made the poem alive and must respond to it appropriately.

By viewing the poem as a living thing, the reader is forced to give it the most adequate interpretation—the special kind outlined in Chapter 3. The key may be found in the notion of freedom. The difference between inanimate and animate objects, particularly human individuals, lies in the freedom of choice which characterizes all the actions of the latter and is absent from the actions of the former: "Man is not a thing to be pushed about. . . . He is a spirit who learns . . . by exercising the freedom which is his being."[26] Only in choosing and pursuing goals does a man develop and realize himself, to become what he truly is. The free individual might best be characterized as a set of possibilities for fulfillment or growth.[27] When Richards regards the poem as alive, he is seeing *it* as a set of possibilities for development. This, indeed, is indicated in his answer, in "The Interactions of Words," to the "poetic" question, "What is a word?": "A word . . . is a permanent set of possibilities of understanding," similar to but radically more complex than Mill's table, the "permanent possibility of sensation."[28] As a set of possibilities, the poem, like a human being, presents the reader with an ever-changing, fluid face. He cannot grasp a single aspect of the poem and think he has understood the real poem any more than he can attribute a single description to the human being and think he has comprehended his nature. Nor

26. "The Future of the Humanities in General Education," *Speculative Instruments*, p. 63.
27. *How To Read a Page*, pp. 174–75, 222, 227.
28. *Language of Poetry*, ed. Tate, p. 73.

can he expect the very probably incompatible combination of the poem's different aspects to exhaust its nature, any more than he can expect the combination of different descriptions of the human being to exhaust his nature. Nevertheless, the only way to come to know the poem (or the human being) is through its multiple faces. Thus the reader finds himself in the puzzling situation—as in his relationships with other men—of having to return to the poem again and again, approaching it in different ways to uncover its different facets, but realizing all the while that it is not exhausted by any one of them or even by their combination.

The parallel between the poem and the human being illuminates some of Richards' most puzzling pronouncements. The re-cognizing of imagination by imagination of *Coleridge,* for instance, is accomplished through the medium of freedom. The poetic question of "The Interactions of Words"—What is a word?—

> has to be its own answer. . . . As an answer it is aware that it is a bundle of possibilities dependent on other possibilities which in turn it in part determines; as a question it is attempting through its influence on them to become more completely itself. It is growing as a cell grows with other cells.[29]

The necessity of viewing the poem from many different perspectives, which is one important corollary of seeing it as alive, provides the theme for Richards' later discussions of the difference between good and bad reading. In "Fifteen Lines from Landor"[30] he offers an account of correctness of reading which contrasts sharply with that of *Principles* which is based

29. Ibid., pp. 72–73.
30. *Speculative Instruments,* pp. 181–97.

on the matching of poet's and reader's experiences. In fact, he seems to attack his own earlier view when he contrasts his new conception with what he deems the ordinary use of "correct" —"which perhaps follows some such definition as 'corresponding' to what was in 'the poet's mind,' "—by suggesting that the new definition has the advantage of not forcing us "even by fiction" to posit dead men's experiences and thus to think that we have a test for correctness of reading when we actually do not *(Speculative Instruments,* pp. 196–97). The new tests for the correctness of an interpretation are

> its internal coherence and its coherence with all else that is relevant. . . . [Or, alternatively] we can say . . . that this inner and outer coherence is the correctness. When an interpretation hangs together (without conflicting with anything else: history, literary tradition, etc.) we call it correct—when it takes into account all the items given for interpretation and orders the other items, by which it interprets them, in the most acceptable manner. (p. 196)

Earlier in the essay Richards has noted that "a first difference between good and bad readers can be stated simply in terms of the number of relevant items that they can bring and hold together as co-operating signs" (pp. 183–84). Among such items he includes the literal senses of words and sentences, the metaphoric senses, feeling, and tone. The internal coherence cited in his new conception of correctness thus seems to be grounded in multiple approaches to the poem. A hint of the magnitude of the change in Richards' depiction of good reading can be seen in his use of the criterion of "internal and external coherence." This test comes close to the description of the results of the synaesthetic experience described in *The Foundations of Aesthetics*—as we become more ourselves, things become more themselves—and is reminiscent of the fruits of self-completion described in *Practical Criticism,* the union of the external and the internal: "Being more at one within itself the mind thereby becomes more appropriately responsive to the outer world" (p. 287). In both cases there is a clear reference to the *value* of the poetic experience. In "Fifteen Lines," Richards does not further develop the idea that correct reading is related in some way to value, but the indication of such a relationship is antithetical to the sharp distinction drawn between value and the tests for adequate communication in *Principles.*

The need for diverse approaches to the poetic passage is stressed also in "Poetry as an Instrument for Research." In Chapter 3, I quoted a passage from this essay which contrasts the fluidity of poetic language with the rigidity of non-poetic language. Richards sees this fluidity as characterizing not only the *meanings* of poetry, but its *words* as well. On one page he defines poetry as "words so used that their meanings are free . . . to dispose themselves";[31] but on the following page he suggests that when we leave certain *words* "free to waltz about with one another as much as they please," we are "talking 'Poetry' [in this special sense] . . . not prose." The easy transition between the fluidity of meanings and of words belies a close relationship between the two: meanings become fluid only when the words of the poem are viewed in many different contexts and combinations.

A late treatment of proper reading, in the "Proem" to *Goodbye Earth and other Poems,*[32] relates Richards' views on correctness and value:

> An account of a poem's structure, however refined and exact it may appear, has still only a limited claim upon

31. *Speculative Instruments,* p. 149.
32. New York, 1958.

the readers to whom it is offered. . . . When is a poem
finished? When is any interpretation of it complete? . . .
Charles Sanders Pierce's doctrine of the extendible in-
terpretant is highly relevant here.

Moreover, the most discussed poet of my time, in his
Minnesota lecture, has justly and refreshingly remarked:
"I suspect, in fact, that a good deal of the value of an
interpretation is—that it should be my own interpretation." Whatever accounts are offered to the reader must
leave him—in a very deep sense—free to choose, though
they may supply wherewithal for exercise of choice.

This is not—dare I note?—any general license to readers to differ as they please or in other ways and over
other points than they must. For this deep freedom in
reading is made possible only by the widest surface conformities: as to how the words in a poem are recognized,
as to how surface (plain sense) meanings are ascribed, as
to how rhythms are followed, allusions caught, cognates
given their weight, metaphors taken in, rhetorical paral-
lelisms and oppositions obeyed and so forth, throughout
all the machinations. (pp. viii–ix)

This extended statement, together with his other comments
on correctness, indicates quite nicely the connections which
Richards sees between the living poem and the special sort of
interpretation demanded by poetry. When the reader regards
a poetic utterance as a living thing, he realizes that it is necessary to adopt many different approaches to it in order to capture
its real nature. That is, he has to see its words as fluid, as related to one another in a variety of ways. The approaches,
which yield differing combinations and configurations of the
words, are summed up in the "external coherence" of "Fifteen
Lines," the suggestions of "history, literary tradition, etc.,"

or even better in the "surface conformities" of the "Proem": "how the words in a poem are recognized," "how surface . . . meanings are ascribed," "how rhythms are followed, allusions caught, cognates given their weight, metaphors taken in." Obedience to these conformities forces the reader to return to the work repeatedly in order to interpret it from different perspectives. In this way, the poem is enriched through the inclusion of more and more meanings. But the animate quality of the work (very likely reflected in the incompatibility of these meanings) indicates that the reader must go even further to discover its true nature. He must view it as a fact of mind, as an occasion for the balancing of purposes, and not as an assertion. This adjustment makes it possible for the reader to choose, for now the poem is important to him from the standpoint of his own development. Thus the relation between correct reading and value, hinted at in "Fifteen Lines," becomes clear, and we see why it is only in obeying the "widest surface conformities" that we gain "deep freedom" to choose.

There are, then, a series of links between appreciating the living quality of the utterance, approaching it in a variety of ways, developing the multiple meanings of the components, seeing the poem as a fact of mind and not as doctrine, and being, then, in a position to evaluate it. In describing the imaginative reading of poetry in Chapter 3, I deferred answering the question: what occasions the special sort of interpretation of poetic language? It should now be clear that the attitude adopted by the reader toward the poem generates his peculiar experience. It should also be apparent why Richards shifted from a non-projective to a projective view in the later works. He had to exclude that interpretation of the communicative scheme which rendered it merely a version of the Vulgar Packaging View. By depicting the poem as alive, he was able to find a place for critical rules consonant with his most adequate views on the reading of poetry.

The projective account of the poem should be understood, then, as complementary to my analysis of poetic language in Chapter 3, not as an alternative to it. Here, I do not purport to describe the reading of a poem from the disinterested viewpoint of the aesthetician, but to describe the nature of the poem from the interested viewpoint of the reader or critic. This description provides no new information about the nature of poetic language, but it does afford the basis for an analysis of the *approach* to the poem. There is a place for negative as well as positive critical rules or statements within this theory. In keeping with Richards' earlier views, respect for the integrity of the living poem demands negative rules which free the reader from irrelevant considerations. Positive rules lead him to the work by calling attention to the surface conformities which must be followed to make choice possible. The statements embodying these positive rules develop the sense of the poem, clarify its allusions, indicate its metaphoric structure, call attention to its rhythmic scheme, and so on, "throughout all the machinations." Since they lead to the proper understanding and evaluation of the poem, both negative and positive critical statements are justified instrumentally; but they are in no way a substitute for the poem. That critical statements function as guides which direct the reader to facets of the work deserving his attention is a familiar view in contemporary critical theory. His setting of this view in the context of the living quality of the poem, however, leads Richards to a rather unusual emphasis on the need for a diversity of such guides. It may even imply that there is positive value in divergent criticisms of a single work.

We shall see in Chapter 6 why Richards is prevented from

117

developing this theory more fully. Even as it stands the account clarifies many of the puzzling hints of a critical theory which existed in *Coleridge*. The relationships between the projective imagination, good sense, and good reading are now comprehensible. Good sense provides the link between projecting meanings into the words of the poem to see it as alive, and the "movements of exploration" and "searchings for meanings" which the reading of good modern verse requires. It serves to direct the reader to the work in such a way that he can judge it as a "whole man."

One remaining major aspect of Richards' theory of literature demands clarification before I shall be able to assess the strengths and weaknesses of the theory as a whole. This is his view on the outcome of reading poetry: the role of poetry in life, particularly its relation to science and morality. Again, his later works provide an improved account of misleading earlier versions of these relationships.

5

The Outcome of Reading Poetry: Poetry, Science, and Morality

> If we would understand the place of the arts in civilisation we must consider them more closely. An improvement of response is the only benefit which anyone can receive, and the degradation, the lowering of a response, is the only calamity.[1]

> The quality of our living . . . is most intimately mixed up with the state of order-disorder within our lexical-structural would-be system. And Poetry . . . is our exemplar of that would-be system at its most entire—being most itself.[2]

Since his earliest works, Richards has argued against the isolation of poetry in a world of its own by stressing the tremendous influence of reading poetry on non-poetic experience. But while his views on the relationship of poetry and life have not changed greatly over the years, he seems, in his early writings, to advocate a different and totally unsatisfactory position

---

1. *Principles,* p. 237.
2. "The Future of Poetry," p. 126.

concerning their relationship. It is another case where Richards' mode of presentation obscures his true views from himself and his readers. This time the main culprit is the "impulse theory of values." In his earlier works Richards seems to advance the truly absurd view that poetry represents the only real hope for mankind. It is certainly not the only idea concerning the relationship of poetry and life expressed in the early books, but it is the one most frequently seized upon by Richards' critics and the one we must consequently analyze, if only to prepare the way for developing his more adequate views. This oversimplified account of the instrumental value of poetry stems from Richards' discussions of poetry and belief, and from his theory of value, both of which I shall review briefly.

In his preface to *The Meaning of Meaning,* Richards states that one of the notorious controversies that can be solved by his distinction of the functions of language into "symbolic" and "emotive" is the controversy between religion and science (pp. xxvi–xxvii). The distinction between symbolic and emotive functions operative here is one which I developed in Chapter 3: the symbolic use of language to communicate thoughts concerning things referred to as contrasted with its emotive use to arouse attitudes. Poetry, as the prime example of the emotive use of language, does not refer to any state of affairs; hence it is inappropriate to apply to the poem any of the tests one applies to referential language. Often poetry relies for its effect upon the reader's *acceptance* (as true) of statements symbolized by its words. This provisional acceptance is justified solely by its effect upon the reader's attitudes; he does not use the statements to learn anything about his environment. Sometimes attitudes aroused in the course of reading are based upon the reader's beliefs. There is no justification for this intrusion of belief into the experience; it merely fixes the attitude and hence endangers it. Sometimes the state of mind or attitude in which the reader finishes the poem is mistaken for a referential state-ment, and the value of the poem is attributed to the truth of this statement. Such confusion can only be misleading.

Chapter XXXV of *Principles,* Chapter VII (Part 3) of *Practical Criticism,* and Chapter VI of *Science and Poetry,* in dif-ferent ways and with varying degrees of success, all make this same point: a poem is not true or false in the way in which any referential statement is true or false. The above description is modeled after that in *Principles.* In *Practical Criticism,* Rich-ards puts the point this way: a doctrine expressed in a poem— he considers religious doctrines primarily—may receive either intellectual or emotional acceptance, and the justification for these two sorts of acceptance differs. A person is justified in accepting a doctrine intellectually if it fits coherently with *all* his other thoughts or ideas; he is justified in accepting it emo-tionally if it satisfies some need or leads to a desirable attitude or feeling. If we subject a doctrine expressed in a poem to the intellectual test, "we have for the moment ceased to be reading poetry and have become astronomers, or theologians, or mor-alists, persons engaged in quite a different type of activity" (p. 277).

The fifth and sixth chapters of *Science and Poetry,* "The Neutralization of Nature" and "Poetry and Beliefs," are two of Richards' best known and most criticized pieces. I would summarize "The Neutralization of Nature" as follows: For ten thousand years man had what Richards calls a "magical view" of the universe. This view enabled him to people the universe with gods and other forces on which he was able to center his emotions and attitudes. Thus for ten thousand years nature supplied a focus and support for man's needs. In the twentieth century, however, this magical view has all but given way to what Richards calls the "scientific view" of the universe. Such a view perhaps affords emotional satisfaction to the scientist, but the grey, cold universe which he describes is of little solace to the ordinary man. There is no god to listen to problems and to offer comfort. In replacing his spurious knowledge of gods and forces by actual knowledge, man has lost all support for his emotions and attitudes. The "biological crisis" has alienated him from his environment; it has set him adrift.

It is important to correct some common misconceptions— shared, for instance, by the average critic of Chapter 1—concerning what Richards is saying here. When he claims that science does not provide satisfactions for man's emotional needs, that it merely indicates how things occur and does not answer the ultimate questions concerning the nature of things, he is not derogating science; he is merely describing its function. Similarly, when he refers to the magical view of the universe as that which supplies answers to "pseudo-questions"— so-called because they are not really demands for knowledge at all but rather requests for assurance—he is not derogating the magical view; he is merely contrasting it with science. It is unfortunate that Richards uses terms with such marked connotations as "ultimate" or "pseudo," but at least thus far he has not come out for or against either the magical (religious) or the scientific position.

In the following chapter, "Poetry and Beliefs," Richards presents a view close to the one we have seen him develop in *Principles* and *Practical Criticism*. Poetry consists largely of pseudo-statements. A pseudo-statement seems to be giving us some information about the world but really is not, just as a pseudo-question seems to be a demand for knowledge but really is not. And, as a pseudo-question is a request for assurance, so the "truth" of a pseudo-statement is measured not by its correspondence with some state of affairs but by the degree to which the statement suits or serves an emotional need of the individual. Pseudo-statements are not less important to us than scientific statements. But while the relevant consequences of scientific statements are unlimited, those of pseudo-statements are limited by their function. The close parallel of "pseudo-statement" and "pseudo-question" allows Richards to use this analysis of poetry to suggest a solution to the problem of man's current alienation, raised in his previous chapter. The remedy to the contemporary situation is to dissociate our ideas "about God, about the universe, about human nature, the relations of mind to mind, about the soul, its rank and destiny" from belief (pp. 71–72).

> Poetry conclusively shows that even the most important among our attitudes can be aroused and maintained without any belief entering in at all. Those of Tragedy, for example. We need no beliefs, and indeed we must have none, if we are to read *King Lear*. (p. 72)

Thus far it seems that the reading of poetry provides a useful example which, when adopted by religion, will provide a way out of the contemporary chaos. At several points in Chapter VI Richards seems to accept the independent status of poetry and religion and to acknowledge the worth of the latter. Our views about God, the soul, and so on, are "pivotal points in the organisation of the mind, vital to its well-being" (p. 71); and, when released from inappropriate belief, they can still be "the main instruments by which we order our attitudes to one another and to the world" (p. 72) and remain, as they were, "as valuable as ever" (p. 79).

But something very peculiar happens in this chapter. Richards does not introduce his poetic analogue as a solution to the problems of religion or morality or outmoded beliefs, but rather as a new way to take "countless pseudo-statements— about God" (p. 71), and so on. That is, his poetic solution is a solution to a problem which he now presents in *linguistic* terms. And what was a supposed conflict between *religion* and science quickly becomes one between *poetry* and science. In showing how that conflict, described in Chapter V, might be eased, Richards has simply allowed poetry to assimilate religion. The easy move from regarding poetry as *suggesting* a solution to man's modern predicament to regarding it as *being* the solution to this predicament rests on two aspects of Richards' thought almost as familiar as the sharp separation between referential and non-referential statements discussed previously. These are his related views on value and the continuity of poetic and non-poetic experience.

The impulse theory of value was first outlined in *Principles* (ch. 7). There Richards defines the valuable as "anything . . . which will satisfy an appetency without involving the frustration of some equal or *more important* appetency" (p. 48). An "appetency" is a seeking-after impulse (as contrasted with an "aversion," a shunning impulse). The "importance" of an impulse is *"the extent of the disturbance of other impulses in the individual's activities which the thwarting of the impulse involves"* (p. 51). Thus, that experience is more valuable which consistently satisfies more appentencies. This theory is a naturalistic version of the traditional "unity-in-variety" theory: the most valuable experience is that which satisfies the most impulses (variety) with the least frustration (unity). This is not a hedonistic theory. There is not even a necessary concomitance of the satisfaction of the greatest number of appetencies with a feeling of pleasure, and certainly the satisfaction cannot be defined in these terms (p. 70).

In *Science and Poetry,* Richards introduces his theory of value in this way: "If the mind is a system of interests, and if an experience is their play, the worth of any experience is a matter of the degree to which the mind, through this experience attains a complete equilibrium" (p. 38). Hypothesizing a person who, though unaware of it, has but one hour to live and whose experience during this hour will have absolutely no effect upon others, Richards asks, "What shall we say it would be best for him, if he could, to do?" (p. 40). His answer is that "the best life then which we can wish for our friend will be one in which as much as possible of himself is engaged (as many of his impulses as possible). And this with as little conflict . . . as there can be. . . . And if it is asked, what does such life feel like, how is it to live through? the answer is that it feels like and is the experience of poetry" (pp. 42–43). It is, in fact, the synaesthetic experience described in *The Foundations of Aesthetics*.

The introduction of the experience of poetry into this discussion of value is not surprising. In his "psychology" in *Principles,* Richards claims, as we have seen above, that any experience is best described in terms of its impulses. There is nothing peculiar, then, about a poem. There is no special world in which it exists. The only important difference between the experience of a poem and any other experience is quantitative. The former is generally "higher" or "more delicately organized" (p. 78) because, simply, there are more impulses unified in it:

> When we look at a picture, or read a poem, or listen to music, we are not doing something quite unlike what we were doing on our way to the Gallery or when we dressed in the morning. The fashion in which the experience is caused in us is different, and as a rule the experience is more complex and, if we are successful, more unified. But our activity is not of a fundamentally different kind. (pp. 16–17)

It is simply a better experience.

Keeping in mind Richards' sharp distinction between emotive and referential uses of language, his theory of value, and his related stress of the continuity of poetry and life, we can easily see how he might have come to consider poetry the remedy for the world's ills. Valuable attitudes rest only upon themselves. "Experience is its own justification."[3] But the most valuable attitudes arise in the reading of poetry, for here we find the most sensitive balancing of impulses. Moreover, "the world of poetry has in no sense any different reality from the rest of the world,"[4] so these are the very attitudes that we are seeking. Poetry can save us because it can provide us with the best experiences, which are their own justification. Richards has so dichotomized life—into an imaginative life (a life of value) and a referential life (a life of fact)—that all ordinary experiences, insofar as they express values, can be viewed as good or bad poetry. He is not just saying that poetry, besides its intrinsic value, has a great instrumental value; he is claiming that poetry's intrinsic value *is* its instrumental value. This is not Richards' real view, but sometimes he writes as though it were:

> There is no such gulf between poetry and life as over-literary persons sometimes suppose. There is no gap between our everyday emotional life and the material of poetry. The verbal expression of this life, at its finest, is forced to use the technique of poetry; that is the only essential difference. We cannot avoid the material of poetry. If we do not live in consonance with good poetry, we must live in consonance with bad poetry.[5]

3. *Science and Poetry*, p. 79.
4. *Principles*, p. 78.
5. *Practical Criticism*, pp. 319–20.

The two problems "What is good?" and "What are the arts?" reflect light upon one another. Neither in fact can be fully answered without the other.[6]

Instead of recognizing that value lies in the "minute particulars" of response and attitude, we have tried to find it in conformity to abstract prescriptions and general rules of conduct. The artist is an expert in the "minute particulars" and *qua* artist pays little or no attention to generalisations which he finds in actual practice are too crude to discriminate between what is valuable and the reverse. . . . The fine conduct of life springs only from fine ordering of responses far too subtle to be touched by any general ethical maxims. . . . Bad taste and crude responses are not mere flaws in an otherwise admirable person. They are actually a root evil from which other defects follow. No life can be excellent in which the elementary responses are disorganised and confused.[7]

At present bad literature, bad art, the cinema, etc., are an influence of the first importance in fixing immature and actually inapplicable attitudes to most things.[8]

Each of the foregoing statements, we shall discover, is ambiguous. But on first glance they seem to follow from the belief that experiences of poetry are our most valuable experiences.

The more extreme of Richards' claims in *Coleridge,* culminating in the view that the poet is to "constitute an order for our minds," stem from the same combination of factors—the distinct emotive-referential split, the impulse theory of value, and the continuity of poetry and life—retained in that book.

6. *Principles,* p. 37.
7. Ibid., pp. 61–62.
8. Ibid., pp. 202–03.

The last theme is stressed in the common origin (in the secondary imagination) of poetry and the world of value. The division between the referential and emotive uses of language is reflected in the distinction of Nature-II and Nature-III, the worlds of fact and value. The impulse theory of value hovers over his discussion of the relative values of imaginative and fanciful poetry.

Alongside this unpromising analysis of the relationship of poetry and life, we find, in the early works and in *Coleridge,* a different and much more adequate theory. To develop this other approach, I can best start with an obvious problem in the simple theory discussed above. The imaginative life may be its own justification, but why should reading poetry provide specific answers to the problems faced by different individuals? Only by ignoring the very divergent problems of different men to concentrate on the problems of contemporary man (as in *Science and Poetry)* can Richards avoid this question. The facts that action is sometimes precisely what is needed in a particular situation and that poetry generates a synaesthetic experience which never leads to action, but rather to an equilibrium of impulses, indicate that the experiences of poetry are not *in themselves* the answers to man's problems. Richards, of course, realizes this point, though sometimes he seems to forget it or to underemphasize its importance. Undoubtedly the ambiguity of the poetic experience which I discussed in Chapter 4 is largely responsible for this. When this experience is viewed as a valuable set of attitudes whose reception depends upon the suppression of the reader's "personal particularities," the importance of his individual predicament will be overlooked. In one of his subtlest discussions—that concerning the "stock response" in *Practical Criticism*—Richards does stress the importance of the individual's responding appropriately to the external situation. He names *withdrawal from experience* as the chief cause of "ill-appropriate, stereotyped reactions" (p. 246). Far from responses being their own justification, they must be justified by the objective situation toward which they are directed. "The only corrective in all cases must be a closer contact with reality, either directly, through experience of actual things, or mediately through other minds which are in closer contact" (p. 251). Richards can, when he wants, de-emphasize the gap between fact and value as much as he emphasizes it at other times!

But if poetry cannot save us simply by providing us with valuable experiences, what is its role in life? Richards offers, in the early books, several statements of a position different from that outlined above. None of them has proven very convincing, however, probably because, thinking that the impulse theory of value made them obvious, he did not bother to develop them clearly. In *Principles,* he quotes Shelley approvingly: "Poetry acts in a diviner manner. It awakens and enlarges the mind itself by rendering it the receptacle of a thousand unapprehended combinations of thought," and he adds that "the enlargement of the mind, the widening of the sphere of human sensibility, is brought about through poetry" (p. 67). "The poets are failing us," he notes in *Science and Poetry,* "if after reading them we do not find ourselves changed . . . with a permanent alteration of our possibilities as responsive individuals in good or bad adjustment to an all but overwhelming concourse of stimulations" (p. 53). The first quotation from *Principles*—cited at the head of this chapter—is in the same vein. This statement concludes a discussion of the "transference effect" of art:

> Finer adjustment, clearer and more delicate accommo-
> dation or reconciliation of impulses in any one field tends
> to promote it in others. . . .

129

> There is abundant evidence that removal of confusion in one sphere of activity tends to be favourable to its removal elsewhere. (p. 234)

Thus, "The results, for good or evil, of the untrammelled response [to poetry] are not lost to us in our usual trafficking" (p. 238). Finally, the statements I quoted earlier in support of Richards' oversimplified view of the relationship between poetry and life may be seen as ambiguously supporting this different view as well. The ambiguity is best illustrated in this statement from *The Meaning of Meaning:* "A poem—or a religion . . . —has no concern with limited and directed reference. . . . It has a different, though an equally important and a far more vital function. . . . What it does, or should do, is to induce a fitting attitude to experience" (p. 270).[9] Poetry induces a fitting attitude toward experience, we might say, because it forces the reader to use in more subtle ways the material presented to him in experience. It makes him more sensitive, more open to different possibilities of response. To arrive at this interpretation we take the word "attitude" in its ordinary sense of "a way of approaching." But we have seen that Richards also uses "attitude" in the special sense of "balance of impulses." With this sense in mind, the statement from *The Meaning of Meaning* supports the oversimplified position discussed above. Poetry's vital function is to induce states of balanced impulses in the reader.

---

9. Richards adds a footnote on "attitude" which seems only to underscore its ambiguity: " 'attitude' should throughout this discussion be understood in a wide sense, as covering all the ways in which impulses may be set ready for action; including those peculiar settings from which no overt action results, often spoken of as the 'aesthetic moods' or 'aesthetic emotions.' "

This ambiguity in the meaning of "attitude" explains why Richards feels it unnecessary in his early works to offer a more complete justification of his view that there is a transference of ability in poetry to other spheres. It may be true, though it is certainly not obvious, that ability in poetry will be transferred to non-poetic situations. But in the early works Richards never really elucidates this ability. We find statements such as this:

> No one who has repeatedly lived through experiences at the level of discrimination and co-ordination presupposed by the greater writers, can ever . . . be contented with ordinary crudities. . . . And conversely, keen and vigilant enjoyment of Miss Dell, Mr Burroughs, Mrs Wilcox or Mr Hutchinson . . . is likely to have as a consequence not only an acceptance of the mediocre in ordinary life, but a blurring and confusion of impulses and a very widespread loss of value.[10]

Is he saying here that reading bad poetry results in an unsatisfactory approach ("attitude" in the ordinary sense) to non-poetic experiences, or that it results in bad responses ("attitude" in his technical sense) and a consequent "loss of value"? Probably he means the former, but the ambiguity explains not only why we find the less satisfactory, oversimplified view expressed so frequently in his early works, but also why he developed his more adequate view so sketchily.

My survey of Richards' earlier discussions of the relationship between poetry and life has presented a confusing and disappointing picture. His rather attractive transference theory is confused with the less attractive, naïve view that poetry can directly cure the world's ills. Even when he is advocating the

10. *Principles,* p. 230.

transference view, however, the lingering effects of the other theory prevent its clear development. Richards' critics have understandably not accepted either view. The first is too extreme; the second too mysterious.

Richards never explicitly abandons the impulse theory of the early works. In *The Philosophy of Rhetoric* he holds that the impulse theory of value serves the negative function of keeping the wrong assumptions from "frustrating and misleading sagacity" (p. 38). In "Emotive Meaning Again" he claims that the attempt in *Principles* "to put the causes, characters, and consequences of a mental event in the place of what is known, felt, and willed . . . was *as science,* I think still, on the right lines."[11] Nevertheless, there is little reliance on this framework in the later works. We might, then, expect a more elaborate defense of his views on the instrumental value of poetry in these works, not simply the obfuscating appeal to impulses. But though Richards is still convinced of the high instrumental value of poetry in his later writings, he seems even less willing to discuss why it is so valuable. In part, this may be attributed to his belief that he had already accounted for this value in the earlier works; in part, to a shifting of his interest away from poetry. I have noted earlier, however, that many of his later writings, though ostensibly not dealing with poetry, actually illuminate his views on this subject. And, indeed, we find in Richards' later discussions of "philosophy" an elaboration of the early transference view.

The problem is posed in *Coleridge.* There Richards found the solution to the problems of metaphysics and morals in Coleridge's theory of poetry. More specifically, the conflict

11. *Speculative Instruments,* p 44n.

between the nature of value and the nature of our ordinary experience—that is, the nature of morality and religion and that of science—is solved by a return to the "fact of mind" from which they both spring, just as the apparent conflict between the realist and projective theories of Coleridge and Wordsworth is solved by such a return. Poetry thus introduces peace in a troubled situation, and there its instrumental value lies. But how does it solve this conflict?

It is clear from *Coleridge* that Richards does not think that the solution is accomplished by poetry's assimilation of either science or value. In poetry "we receive but what we give" while our response to the scientific myth must be complete. And poetry which leads to "suasion to a policy . . . or some temporary or permanent exclusive attitude to the world" (p. 213) has only a subordinate value. These are later versions of views clearly expressed in *Principles*. Poetic statement is not scientific statement; nor does poetry support particular responses, but rather makes the individual more sensitive and flexible. My investigation of Richards' account of the reading of poetry further supports this separation of poetry from both science and morality. The poem is untranslatable; it *absorbs* the individual in the purposes which underlie its varied frameworks, rather than supporting any particular purpose. Poetry is, then, distinct from both science and value and must resolve their conflict as a third party. The clue to the mode of resolution may be found in Richards' later essays, particularly those appearing in *Speculative Instruments*. Many of the pieces collected in this book are devoted to describing conflicts and suggesting ways of ending them. The conflicts discussed include those among persons and nations, but Richards seems particularly fascinated by those among academic disciplines.[12]

12. See, esp., the following pieces in *Speculative Instruments:* "Foreword," pp. ix-xii; "Notes toward an Agreement between Literary Criti-

This is not surprising when we realize that the conflict between the sciences and the humanities is but the latest Richardsian version of the conflict between science and value.

Richards frequently depicts the conflict between these disciplines as a struggle between the different language functions—referential and emotive.[13] It is in a discussion of the relationships and mediation between these functions, then, that we find an important clue to the instrumental value of poetry in the late essay, "Emotive Meaning Again." There Richards suggests that the clarification of the relationships between the emotive and referential uses of language might best be accomplished by a poetic account, the sort of clarification "which a play rather than an essay might offer" *(Speculative Instruments,* p. 40). The instrument which is needed to illumine the relationships of the different functions of language must be neither a "referential account" of the two sorts of meaning nor "a sermon, as eloquent as we can make it, on man's duties to God and man." The first "sacrifices emotive meaning by example," and the second "seems unlikely, at this juncture, to be either forthcoming or effective." Rather,

> this instrument must be able to mediate, it must have a foot in each boat and yet be run away with by neither. And yet again, it must leave both functions free, in the sense that it is their creature and has no support or authority which does not derive in the end from them. It can be no more than an agency through which they may keep them-

cism and Some of the Sciences," pp. 3–16; "The Idea of a University," pp. 107–12; "Toward a More Synoptic View," pp. 113–26; "Language and Value," pp. 137–45. Also see I. A. Richards, *Nations and Peace* (New York, 1947).

13. See, e.g., "Emotive Language Still," *Yale Review, 39* (1949), 115–18; "Emotive Meaning Again," *Speculative Instruments,* pp. 54–56.

selves from illegitimate mutual interference. . . . To distinguish, relate, and mediate between the modes of language . . . we need no more than, and no less than, Philosophy. (pp. 49–50)

This is not the first occasion on which Richards associates philosophy with the mediation of conflict. In *Mencius* he contrasts the "long drawn out and still drawn struggle between Aristotelianism and Platonism, or the beautiful specimens of mutual misunderstanding that any controversy between Oxford and Cambridge logicians of the last generation will provide" with the "strange peace in philosophy" which would ensue if philosophers would become aware of the purposive nature of all thinking and practice multiple definition (pp. 90, 93).

The three suggestions of this passage—that philosophy properly practiced concerns itself with the various meanings of words, that it is closely occupied with purposes, and that it should lead not to dispute but to deep understanding—are unfortunately subject to the confusion which undercuts Richards' discussions of multiple meaning. I noted in Chapter 3 that Richards uses many of these discussions as opportunities for revealing the diverse organizational frameworks which underlie all utterances. Thus, in *How To Read a Page,* he contrasts Christian and Platonic conceptions of love, and Lockean and Platonic views of knowledge, in his discussions of the words "love" and "idea" (pp. 153–56, 191–203). But these ambiguous concepts have only an indirect connection, as I noted, with the multiplicity of meanings of most isolated words, the factor which is centrally responsible for the peculiar nature of poetic language. This confusion in his use of "multiple meaning" makes it difficult to know precisely what Richards is attributing to philosophy here. Is he making the rather trite claim that philosophers will stop arguing when they realize that their

135

opponents and they, because of their different purposes, orga-
nize their experience in accordance with different frameworks?
Or is he claiming that philosophy should concern itself directly
with the sort of multiple meaning one encounters, for instance,
in an imaginative poem?

Probably he has both points in mind in *Mencius*. In later
works, however, where he stresses the peculiar nature of the
philosophic enterprise, he excludes the first interpretation.
It is not open to the philosopher simply to accept alternative
formulations of problems and their solutions while pursuing
in detail his own particular concerns. His job consists, rather,
in the mediation and unification of the different approaches.
The task of the perfect dialectician of *How To Read a Page,*
for example, is to create a "mediating philosophy" which would
relate the different questions asked by "different philosophies"
(pp. 172–73). Richards' dialectician, like the Platonic philosopher of the *Republic* after whom he is explicitly modeled, is
"able to see the different sciences together as a whole. . . .
Each science . . . simplifies by abstracting. . . . It is this which
separates them. If the body of knowledge they together compose is to be seen as a whole, these abstract simplifications must
be put together again" (p. 215).

This description of the task of philosophy would be very
difficult to understand were it not for our study of Richards'
views on the interpretation of poetry. With these views in
mind, however, we discover that each of the dimensions of
philosophy properly practiced, which Richards outlines in
Mencius, echoes one of the characteristics of poetic language.
The concern with multiple meanings parallels the growth of
meaning of the poetic passage; the centrality of purposes reflects the untranslatability of the poetic passage, explained
by the reader's absorption in the purposes underlying its diverse
frameworks; and the deep understanding in philosophy recalls

the completeness or breadth of the poem. I do not suggest that it is useful to regard philosophy as a poetic enterprise. In fact, I think it is a poor way, one which is bound to lead to the obscurities of *Speculative Instruments*. Nevertheless, it is helpful to see that this is the way in which Richards often represents philosophy in his later works—as something which is more like a play than an essay. As soon as we grasp the similarity of philosophy and poetry, we are afforded additional material for interpreting his literary theory. In particular, an understanding of the way in which Richards takes philosophy to accomplish its task will show how poetry mediates the conflict between the nature of science and the nature of morality, and will thus help us to explain its instrumental value.

Richards' references to philosophy are often merely demands for a study which will settle conflicts between the disciplines. Thus in "Language and Value," he says:

> In setting up an opposition . . . between Science and Religion, what do you think you are doing? Is *this* activity Science or Religion, or a mixture, or neither? . . . This question: "What are we doing?" MOST needs to be asked about our attempts to answer it.
>
> This is (or should be) the perennial embarrassment of Philosophy: it must PRETEND it knows how to behave even while seemingly inquiring into how it ought to behave.
>
> This embarrassment . . . is really the throne: the charge and the task—that of inventing . . . a Supreme Ruler in us which can be justified by its ability to unite under itself, BE in itself, the interests which, without such a Ruler, war with one another in shifting alliances for ever.[14]

14. *Speculative Instruments,* pp. 141–42.

Sometimes, however, he offers hints concerning the way in which the conflict can be ended. The key lies in the purposive nature of all the endeavors of man.[15] Keeping different activities "from illegitimate mutual interference" is accomplished by grasping and integrating the purposes which underlie them. Philosophy accomplishes its job, he indicates in "Toward a More Synoptic View," by showing that all our diverse endeavors and all our different studies (the linguistic reflections of these endeavors) are radically normative.[16] The discovery that purpose is common to all our activities leads to peace between and within the different endeavors. Philosophy, "the diplomatic agency of dialectic, . . . has to *protect* studies from the interferences of other studies, yes. But it has more to do. It has also to help studies out of *self*-frustrations due to their ignorance of what other studies can and should do for them."[17] This synoptic study would have, he states in "The Idea of a University":

> *authority:* an authority which would have behind it *all* that man knows in *all* his modes of knowing and *all* that he would will to become through *all* his quests for being, . . . an authority which could wholly be respected and accepted, because it would represent the whole man, not any party or pressure group among his interests.[18]

Philosophy is obviously a peculiar sort of study, having no interest of its own, but merely "BEing" the varied interests which it controls. It cannot be concerned with purpose, then, as a subject demanding theoretical examination, but must be concerned with it in some other fashion. Again, without the help

15. *How To Read a Page,* p. 227.
16. *Speculative Instruments,* pp. 122–24.
17. Ibid., p. 124.
18. Ibid., p. 112.

of Richards' ideas on the reading of poetry, this would be very mysterious. But the notion of an indirect involvement with purpose, through concern with the varied frameworks underlying the interpretation of an utterance, is by now one familiar to us.

With this help, we might represent the accomplishment of philosophy in this way: philosophy unites diverse studies, such as the sciences and the humanities—the linguistic formulations of man's factual and valuative endeavors—by relating them in such a way as to emphasize the purposive element underlying them all. In doing this, philosophy does not replace these studies, but only enables them to develop fully and freely. In this way philosophy exists for these studies; it *is* "those interests."

Since philosophy is viewed by Richards as a poetic endeavor, we can now see how he views the instrumental value of poetry. Poetry solves the conflict between the nature of science and the nature of value by its emphasis on the common core of these two natures, the purposes which lie behind their development. By being the "exemplar" of our "lexical-structural would-be system . . . at its most entire," it forces us to be more sensitive to the purposes underlying all our endeavors. Poetry is, of course, different from philosophy in that it does not exist solely to lessen the conflicts between our various endeavors but has an intrinsic value of its own. Richards' discussion of philosophy helps us, however, to fill in the undeveloped notion of transference in the early works. What is transferred from the reading of poetry to our non-poetic experiences is a sensitivity for and concern with purpose, upon which is based the overall compatibility of our varied interests and, just as important, our successful advance in each of them.

Richards' early transference view, when elaborated in the light of these recent discussions of philosophy, is certainly superior to his depiction of poetry as the cure for all the world's ills. It is also an improvement on his discussion of the instrumental value of poetry in *Coleridge*. There we find, in Chapter VIII, a hint of this theory; but though his descriptions of the location of the imaginative moment on the "boundary of the mythical" and of the way it forces us to "return to the fact of mind" and to "grow" in it are not without metaphoric appeal, they call for the greater precision which his discussions of philosophy afford.

These three chapters have been devoted to a detailed analysis of Richards' notions of the activity of reading poetry, the approach to poetry, and the outcome of reading poetry. By using materials from his other writings, I have been able to elaborate the ideas implicit in *Coleridge on Imagination* into a complex theory of literature, at which I should now like to take a close critical look.

6

Richards' Theory of Literature: A Critical Appraisal

Richards has not made it easy to determine the precise nature of his theory of literature. Quite the contrary, his approach raises many obstacles to its clear development. It is largely in spite of Richards that I discriminated the concerns of the aesthetician from those of the critic and reader. Serious ambiguities weaken his developed theory as well as his earlier writings, including the confusion of the distinctions between fluid and rigid language and of his two uses of the term "multiple meaning." Richards' use of Wordsworth's *Prelude* in "The Future of Poetry" to discuss imaginative projection, and his numerous comments on philosophy provide good examples of the annoying coyness and obscurity of the later writings. And, most frustrating of all, he seems to accept an instrumental justification of theory, according to which theory best serves its function by multiplying confusions to such a degree that the reader is forced to puzzle them out for himself.

Encounters with these many interpretive obstacles have complicated my task. Nonetheless, I am confident that now Richards' theory of literature is before us. (Thinking it more worthwhile to devote my attention to a re-examination of Richards' writings, I have not explicitly discussed any pub-

141

lished criticisms of Richards, but the most exhaustive analysis and criticism of his works to date, W. H. N. Hotopf's *Language, Thought, and Comprehension,* is described in Appendix 1 [pp. 169–71]). In this final chapter I shall take a critical look at this theory, particularly with a view to isolating the more important gaps and difficulties encountered and to suggesting some possible directions for development and improvement. To set the stage for this critical appraisal, I shall first contrast the developed theory with that outlined by the average critic of Chapter 1, then raise some detailed and general criticisms of the theory and offer some answers to them.

The multiple meaning theory of literature developed in the last four chapters rests upon one basic theoretical insight: poetic language demands a multiple meaning interpretation. The theory developed from this insight relates activity, approach, and outcome, to purposes. In the activity of reading a poem, the reader is involved with purposes by its multiple meanings, its untranslatability, and its completeness. This involvement with purposes is assured by approaching poems as living organisms. One outcome of reading poetry in this way is the focusing of the reader's attention on the purposes underlying non-poetic endeavors. The coherence of this theory contrasts sharply with the picture drawn by the average critic of Chapter 1. Although Richards so interprets his theoretical starting points that they form a fairly consistent whole, there are no obvious connections between the communicative framework, the reduction of the poem to impulses in the nervous system, the distinction between emotive and referential language, and the preferential theory of value. Undoubtedly the average critic's dissatisfactions gain plausibility from this fragmentation; he can attack the theory piecemeal.

142

When viewed in the context of the whole corpus of Richards'
writings, however, the early views prove more secure from
attack. One way in which these earlier views might be strength-
ened is, as I have shown, through the discovery of an ambiguity
in them which allows a more acceptable interpretation. Thus
the "communication of an experience" can be interpreted
either as the passive reception by the reader of a completely
articulated reaction of the poet's or as the occasion for an
active re-creation by the reader. Similarly, a "balance of attitudes" can refer either to a completed psychological state or
to the active endeavor to fix such a state. In each case, the first
interpretation leads to serious difficulties; the second, closely
allied with Richards' multiple meaning theory, seems more
adequate. Another way I have rescued an early view is to show
that it represents only part of a complex idea which Richards
is trying to convey. For example, neither the characterization
of emotive language as non-referential nor its description as
language which arouses attitudes should be taken to be self-
sufficient. Rather, as shown above, these two facets of language should be combined. A third way of solving an apparent
difficulty is through distinguishing, as I have done, between the
very diverse problems confronting the different individuals
concerned with poetry. We can, for instance, answer the criticism that the reduction of a poem to impulses does away with
the poem by suggesting that the poem in question here is only
the poem of the aesthetician, not that of the critic or reader.
The last suggestion is rather strained, however, and indicates
the limits of these attempts to save the early views. The natural
retort in each case will be: But why didn't he avoid the ambiguity, or warn us of the partial nature of the idea, or tell us
about these different interests? Thus, although the early works
may be more misleading than they are wrong, Richards can
nonetheless be criticized for them.

The reinterpretation of Richards' early views in the light of his work as a whole blunts many of the criticisms which the average critic aimed at him. There is, in the multiple meaning theory, no sharp break between attitudes and references and no reduction of the poem to a set of mysterious impulses in the experiencer's nervous system. The uniqueness of the poem is actually supported by Richards' views on the special mode of interpretation of poetic language. Some features of Richards' writings which were criticized by the average critic would seem, however, to be preserved in the multiple meaning theory. Thus, although there is now a clear recognition of the role of the reader's beliefs in supplying a framework for interpretation—arriving at interpretations depends upon his being able to discover frameworks underlying the utterance—there still seems to be no place for considerations of truth in poetry. Richards' claims for poetry are still highly exaggerated, and his views on science, morality, and religion oversimplified. Criticisms of these features linger, then, as criticisms of the multiple meaning theory. As we shall discover, however, they are by no means the most serious difficulties that this theory faces. But before turning to criticism, I must emphasize that even if the theory turns out to be inadequate in minor respects, the central observation on which it turns—the differentiation of poetic from non-poetic language in terms of its mode of interpretation—is a tremendously fruitful one. It may well form the basis, as I shall later suggest, not only for a theory of literature, but for a general aesthetic theory as well. If he had done nothing more than make this single suggestion, Richards' contribution would still have been a truly significant one.

I shall not attempt here to raise every possible objection to Richards' theory, but shall suggest only its most striking weaknesses and point out ways in which they might be corrected. I could effectively do more than this only by comparing Richards' theory with a counter theory of my own, and this is not the appropriate place for such an undertaking. Before raising serious criticisms, however, I must explain why I do not consider some other, fairly obvious criticisms to be very damaging and why, consequently, I do not try to answer them.

Richards' context theory of meaning and his characterization of science are crucial to his developed theory. So, too, at least in modified form, is his preferential theory of values. Each of these facets of Richards' thought has given rise to deserved critical disapproval.[1] They simply will not do as philosophical analyses of meaning, science, or value. It is perhaps enough to remark that each of these analyses is hopelessly out of date. They gain nothing from important contemporary developments in semantics, the philosophy of science, the theory of value, or the theory of knowledge. Richards continually confuses problems of interpretation with problems of meaning. Where he is concerned with meaning, his "substitute" theory begs more questions than it solves and is totally inadequate for

1. See, e.g., Bertrand Russell, "The Meaning of Meaning," *Dial, 81* (1926), 114–21; Thomas C. Pollock, "A Critique of I. A. Richards' Theory of Language and Literature," *A Theory of Meaning Analyzed,* Monograph III, General Semantics Monographs, ed. M. Kending (Chicago, 1942); Max Black, "Some Objections to Ogden and Richards' Theory of Interpretation," *Journal of Philosophy, 39* (1942), 281–90; George Gentry, "Reference and Relation," *Journal of Philosophy, 40* (1943), 253–61; Manuel Bilsky, "I. A. Richards' Theory of Value," *Philosophy and Phenomenological Research, 14* (1954), 536–45; W. H. N. Hotopf, *Language, Thought, and Comprehension, A Case Study in the Writings of I. A. Richards* (Bloomington, 1965), chs. 8, 9; R. S. Crane, "I. A. Richards on the Art of Interpretation," *Ethics, 59* (1949), 112–26; J. G. Spaulding, "Richards' Theory of Poetic Value," *A Theory of Meaning Analyzed,* Monograph III, General Semantics Monographs, ed. M. Kending (Chicago, 1942), pp. 26–35.

non-referential and formal discourse.[2] His view of science is, despite his distinction in *Coleridge* between Nature-III (the world of ordinary experiences) and Nature-IV (the world of physics), pedestrian. Science, for Richards, is practically synonymous with any relatively factual, non-valuative description of environment. It has little to do with the construction of theories and other special activities of persons we call scientists, but must rather be taken in its original sense of "factual knowledge." Finally, his facile justification of his preferential theory of value in terms of preference fares badly in light of recent subtle analyses of the justification of ethical theories by analytic philosophers.[3]

I do not mean to belittle Richards' work in these non-aesthetic areas. His (and Ogden's) psychological theory of meaning heralded a new approach to the field of semantics—in many ways still the most promising approach. His attack on Moore's non-naturalistic ethical theory in *Principles* is brilliant (ch. 6), and, again, satisfaction theories are still among the most powerful contenders in contemporary discussions of ethics. Nevertheless, one would be ill-advised to go to Richards' work to gain insights into these areas; it is simply too dated.

The case is quite otherwise with his insights into problems of literary theory. Here our interest in Richards is not merely historical but contemporary. I shall note below some aspects of his theory of literature which are weakened by his blindness to contemporary philosophic developments. But, in the main, I do not think that he has suffered in this respect. After all, one need not be a philosopher of science, language, or value to do

2. See, e.g., Charles L. Stevenson, *Ethics and Language* (New Haven, 1944), ch. 3; Roderick M. Chisholm, "Intentionality and the Theory of Signs," *Philosophical Studies, 3* (1952), 56–63.

3. See, e.g., R. M. Hare, *The Language of Morals* (Oxford, 1952), ch. 4.

exciting work in aesthetics. Richards requires for his literary theory a theory of interpretation with which he can locate the broad contrast between poetic and non-poetic interpretation, not a theory of meaning. He needs a commonsensical contrast between our poetic and non-poetic activities, not an insight into the activities of specialists such as scientists. Finally, he needs to recognize that we all place values on features of our environment; he need not engage in an intricate discussion of the philosophical bases of these valuations. His theories of meaning, science, and value do serve his requirements.

Some other fairly obvious criticisms come from an opposite quarter. The practicing critic or reader may dismiss Richards' theory of literature because it seems to be too far removed from actual works of art. Such criticisms take two forms: first, there is the complaint that Richards talks in general terms about poetry, but does not discuss any particular poems; second, there is the claim that he does not offer the critic any definite rules or other tools to use in the analysis of poetry. Initially, the first complaint seems to be mistaken. There is actually a large amount of specific critical writing in the Richardsian corpus. Some of this may be found in the better known works. There is, for example, an appendix to *Principles* devoted to an analysis of Eliot's poetry; the seventh chapter of *Science and Poetry,* "Some Contemporary Poets," contains criticisms of the poetical works of Hardy, de la Mare, Yeats, and Lawrence; and *Practical Criticism* is filled with comments on particular poems.[4] Some of the most incisive critical writing, however, appears in little-known periodical pieces written in the 1920's and early 1930's, such as "Gerard Hopkins," "God of Dostoievsky," and "Passage to Forster." In addition, we find detailed attention to literary works in such later pieces as "The

4. Pp. 63, 83, 160, 168–69, 173–76, 193–204, 214–16, 244, 262–70.

Interactions of Words," *"Troilus and Cressida* and Plato," Richards' "Introduction" to *The Portable Coleridge,* "The Sense of Poetry: Shakespeare's 'The Phoenix and the Turtle,' " and "Coleridge's Minor Poems." Nevertheless, the objection carries some weight, for none of this critical writing is integrated into the aesthetic theory. Sometimes, as with the essays on Forster, Dostoievsky, and Coleridge's minor poems, Richards seems merely to be trying to say illuminating things about individual works of art. More frequently, as in his analyses of the "modern" poets, Eliot, and the poetry of Coleridge in *The Portable Coleridge,* he seems to be using literary works to support basic elements of his literary theory (the neutralization of nature and divorce of emotive and referential belief in the first two essays, and the nature of the imagination in the third). Richards' third approach, which we find in the analysis of Donne's "First Anniversary" in "Interactions of Words," or in his analyses of Shakespeare's *Troilus and Cressida* and "The Phoenix and the Turtle," is to use the literary work largely as an occasion for commenting on diverse philosophical theories. Illuminating as these different approaches may be, none indicates how Richards' theory *applies* to particular works.

Nevertheless, I do not think that this constitutes a serious weakness in Richards' theory. He does afford a few examples —including the lines from *Venus and Adonis* and Coleridge's "Dejection"—to illustrate his theory, and, just as important, he suggests many other works, such as Shakespeare's "The Phoenix and the Turtle," Donne's "Nocturnall upon S. Lucie's Day," Keats' "Ode to a Grecian Urn," and Shakespeare's Sonnet LXVI, which the reader himself may view in terms of the theory.[5]

5. See *Principles,* pp. 214, 250; *Mencius on the Mind,* pp. 116–17; "Emotive Language Still," *Yale Review, 39* (1949), 114–15. I might add that Richards devoted a course he once offered at Harvard University to a study of these and similar works. In discussing the poems, Richards

The second criticism—that Richards does not offer the critic any rules by which to analyze poetry—is more quickly dispelled. We cannot blame Richards for offering no rules for the practicing critic, because this is not the function of a theory of literature. He does tell us what kinds of things should be avoided in reading poetry (such as the stock response) and what is the goal of reading it. He further suggests that the critic can say illuminating things about the sense and metaphoric meanings of a poem. It is up to the critic to learn the craft of effecting these goals through his critical comments. Richards does not, however, profess to teach this craft.

Discounting, then, obvious but largely irrelevant criticisms which might be offered by those unfamiliar with the provenance of an aesthetic theory, I find two important specific shortcomings in Richards' theory as well as one very serious general weakness which seems to affect every phase of the theory. The first specific shortcoming undercuts Richards' account of criti-

---

implicitly stressed several facets of the literary theory I here attribute to him. Thus he was particularly concerned with the ambiguity of the word "forbeare" in line 50 of Donne's "Ecstasie" ("desist from" or "put up with") and saw this ambiguity as reflecting the divergent Platonic and physicalistic organizational frameworks underlying the poem. His choice of Sonnet XCIV for intensive study perhaps was dictated by the Greek and Christian conceptions of love—indicated in the images of the unmoved mover of the first lines and the lilies of the last—which are in tension here. I should hasten to add that Richards never explicitly developed these themes. His approach in the course was characteristically non-directional. He rarely offered his own analyses of these poems but, as in *Practical Criticism,* he asked the members of the class to analyze them, then collected and presented the resultant "protocols," with a few provocative comments. Richards' theory is not, I think, one developed in a vacuum. He simply leaves it up to his readers, as he did to his students, to determine its applicability.

cism. It is another case of his refusing to separate the very diverse interests of different individuals concerned with art. This time the confusion is between the reader and the critic. The second specific shortcoming is Richards' continuing exaggeration of the instrumental value of poetry. The serious general weakness I have in mind is the narrowness of Richards' theory, which seems applicable to only a small segment of what is usually considered literature. I shall elaborate each of these criticisms.

My account of Richards' theory of the evaluation of poetry —the theory of "choice"—stresses the subjective nature of evaluation. We frequently find an appeal, however, to an objective basis of evaluation in Richards' works. "To bring the level of popular appreciation nearer to the consensus of best qualified opinion . . . is essential."[6] *"For a good future* poetry *needs a good audience.* Its present audience is, I fear, very small and very poor; indeed, highly incompetent."[7] To some extent these statements merely amount to a plea for better reading and do not represent appeals to specially qualified judges. A poem cannot be properly evaluated if the reader fools himself concerning his own developing needs. Hence the demand for a good audience is sometimes nothing but a demand for a *sincere* audience. In an interesting discussion in *Practical Criticism* (pp. 283–91), based, like the description of synaesthesis, on the *Chung Yung* of Confucius, Richards defines sincerity as "obedience to that tendency which 'seeks' a more perfect order within the mind" (p. 288). Although he manifests an unjustified faith in this tendency—especially the faith that it will hit upon some undeniable tests or touchstones for sincerity—this plea for a sincere audience is compatible with the

6. *Principles,* p. 36.
7. "The Future of Poetry," *Screens,* p. 127.

subjectivism of his account of evaluation. Richards does list five specific tests for sincerity which might be thought to represent a move in the direction of an objective basis of evaluation, but the list is more appropriately taken as indicating *examples* of tests, which may or may not appeal to the reader. Each individual will presumably find himself at a different stage of development and thus will develop different tests reflecting his unique needs.

Sometimes, however, Richards seems to be appealing to a specially qualified judge. In his discussion of bad poetry in *Principles,* he says of a sonnet by Emma Wheeler Wilcox: "The strongest objection to, let us say, the sonnet we have quoted, is that a person who enjoys it, through the very organization of his responses which enables him to enjoy it, is debarred from appreciating many things which, if he could appreciate them, he would prefer" (p. 204). He notes that even a good critic might misjudge the sonnet if he were "at a sufficiently low ebb of neural potency." But while this good critic would correct his judgment "when vigilance was restored, . . . a reader who, at a high degree of vigilance, thoroughly enters into and enjoys this class of verse, is necessarily so organized that he will fail to respond to poetry" (p. 204).

The obvious conflict between the objectivism of this passage and the subjectivism of Richards' general account can be avoided if a distinction is drawn between the activity of the reader and that of the critic, and between what I shall call the "private" poem and the "public" poem with which each is respectively concerned. Richards himself offers a hint toward such a solution shortly following the passage quoted. The observation expressed in the passage constitutes one reason, he suggests, "why indulgence in verse of this character should be condemned" (p. 205). The sort of evaluation to which he is referring here—calling the sonnet "bad" so that readers will not attend to it—is radically different from the evaluation by the reader described as "choice." When the critic calls the sonnet "bad," he is not claiming that it does not meet *his* needs, but rather he is directing potential readers away from it to consider poetry of another character. With the distinction of these two different sorts of evaluation—one concerned with the future growth of the individual reader, the other with the reading activities of a group of persons—there is a place for Richards' emphasis on both subjectivism and objectivism. It is possible, as Richards comments, to "like the 'wrong' poems . . . for reasons which are excellent."[8] But they are presumably called "wrong" in the first place to guide readers to more predictably worthwhile experiences.

Richards never explicitly draws this distinction between the public and the private poem to identify the poem about which he is speaking. The critic, he asserts in *Principles,* must value the poem not simply in terms of his own reactions, but also in terms of the expected reactions of other people: "His judgment is only of general interest in so far as it is representative and reflects what happens in a mind of a certain kind, developed in a certain fashion" (p. 223). But in "Fifteen Lines from Landor," Richards states that

> Every critical opinion is an ellipsis; . . . Fully expanded it would state that if a mind of a certain sort, under certain conditions (stage of its development, width of its recoverable experience, height of its temporary vigilance, direction of its temporary interest, etc.), has, at scores, or hundreds, or thousands of points in the growth of its response to certain words, taken certain courses; then such and such.[9]

8. *Practical Criticism,* p. 349.
9. *Speculative Instruments,* p. 195.

Obviously the latter sort of "critical opinion" is nothing but the report of an individual's experience, and does not purport, as does the first, to be of general interest. Often it is difficult to determine which poem he has in mind. In the same chapter in *Principles* in which he claims that the poem is nothing but a set of words on paper, Richards notes that the critic often "affirms that the effect in his mind is due to special particular features of the object. In this case he is pointing out something about the object in addition to its effect upon him, and this fuller kind of criticism is what we desire" (p. 23). It is unclear whether such a critic would be reporting a private experience, describing an object available to all, or both.

This lack of a clear distinction between the public and the private poem accounts for the gaps in Richards' critical theory. Just as he does not recognize important differences between the critic's and the reader's *evaluation* of a poem, he does not appreciate important differences between the critic's and the reader's *description* of the poem. He sees that the reader's adherence to "surface conformities" is important, but does not examine in any detail the ways in which critical statements force this adherence. Thus his literary theory can first be criticized for its inadequate treatment of the nature and justification of critical statements.

The second specific shortcoming of Richards' theory is that, even in his developed views, poetry is depicted as a panacea for the world's ills. It is certainly true that openness, flexibility, and consideration of purpose are essential to important developments in science and morality. Just as crucial to the growth of these endeavors, however, is decisiveness and commitment. It is important, as Richards stresses, that there be an activity which exhibits, in a non-theoretical fashion, the common normative basis of the sciences and the humanities, of fact and value. Such an activity may help us become tolerant of other

approaches and flexible in our own approach. But this openness and flexibility will not solve the problems of the world.
Thus, even if transference were perfect, poetry, in itself, would
provide no such solutions.

The marked difference between the central value of poetry
and the values of science and morality is reflected in the very
different natures of poetic and other utterances. A poetic utterance may almost be said to "mean" the process of its interpretation, but in a scientific utterance or an evaluative utterance,
the process must be eliminated from the final meaning, however crucial it may be in determining that meaning. At the
close of *Interpretation in Teaching,* Richards sounds the hope
that our ethics, our religion, and even our science might come
close to the condition of the best poetry, whose utterances
must be viewed in the optative mode, not the indicative mode
(pp. 393–94). But this hope is surely one which neither
Richards nor anyone else can really want to come true. It
evinces an indecisiveness which would make life unbearably
dreary.

The serious general weakness of Richards' multiple meaning theory is its narrowness. How can it be called a theory of
literature when it is concerned only with poetry? Further, a
consideration of *Coleridge on Imagination,* where the entire
theory is sketched, immediately suggests that it may be in-
correct even to call it a theory of *poetry,* for there it does not
seem to apply to fanciful poetry, which at first glance appears
very like the rigid language of mathematics, the meanings of
whose elements do not shift in different contexts. In fancy, the
"meanings of the separate words are almost completely auton-
omous . . . " (p. 81); they are "apprehended as though independent of their fellow-members (as they would be if they
belonged to quite other wholes) . . ." (pp. 86–87). The picture
changes, however, as we read more closely. Richards demands

the reader's active interpretation of the fanciful passage in terms of purposes. Thus he indicates that the discovery of certain connections between elements of a fanciful poem would constitute a "strained reading which the context does not invite"; that these connections would be "irrelevant and merely distracting" (pp. 79–80). He notes that the stressing of certain characteristics of the parts is accomplished in fancy "by the final effect, which ruthlessly excludes all but a limited number of interactions between the parts, setting strict frontiers of relevance about them" (p. 92). Nevertheless, if such statements rescue fancy from the status of mathematics, they do not afford it the status of imaginative poetry. Fanciful poetry is assertorial and thus rigid in a crucial respect.

Throughout his works Richards contrasts different sorts of poetry. In *Principles,* he contrasts poetry that depends upon inclusion of impulses with that which depends upon their exclusion (p. 249); in *Rhetoric,* he claims that on a scale whose extremes are fluidity and rigidity, the fluid extreme is "poetry —... some forms of poetry rather" (p. 48). In "The Future of Poetry," he introduces another scale, this time one of the *translatability* of utterances. At one end are those utterances, "sciences," where the "precipitate" ("what can be translated . . . without change") is all that matters. "At the other end is the sort of poetry for which there is either no precipitate . . . or what there is . . . is trivial, negligible. In between there are all sorts of poetry."[10]

Richards also frequently contrasts different poetic structures: poems, for instance, in which imagery or thought is relevant or irrelevant. But his comments on these differences —"A dog is not a defective kind of cat, nor is Swinburne a defective kind of Hardy";[11] "All poetry . . . *can* of course be

10. *Screens,* pp. 122–23.
11. *Principles,* p. 130.

looked on as dramatic; but some poems more invite such reading than others and when so read are best understood,"[12] —suggest the necessity of the different *approaches* demanded by different poems, not necessarily different values in the poems.

Richards equivocates concerning the respective values of these different sorts of poetry. Sometimes he indicates that each sort has its own value. Of art that depends on exclusion, he comments, in *Principles:* "And such art has its own value and its place in human affairs" (p. 249). In *Coleridge,* he quotes Coleridge's line: "Do not let us introduce an Act of Uniformity against poets" in defending the worth of some fanciful lines (p. 95). Just as often, however, he hints that the different sorts of poetry are not on a par. I showed in Chapter 2 how he is indecisive in *Coleridge* concerning the relative worth of imaginative and fanciful poems. But in that work he explicitly distinguishes the "best" poetry—poetry with no ends —from inferior poetry. Perhaps most clearly indicative of his higher esteem for imaginative poetry is Richards' tendency, having distinguished the different sorts of poetry, as in the passage cited from "The Future of Poetry" above, to forget the distinction almost immediately and to use the word "poetry" to refer to imaginative poetry alone.[13]

This equivocation is confusing, but even more perplexing are Richards' shifting positions on the differences between different sorts of poetry. In *Coleridge,* he argues forcefully that the distinction between fancy and imagination is not simply one of degree, but one of kind. However, his reliance on series, spectra, and ranges in his various discussions of the rigid and fluid uses of language and the translatability of utterances presup-

12. *Coleridge,* p. 208.
13. See, e.g., *Screens,* pp. 123–24.

poses a distinction of degree. As with his confusions of the different senses of "fluidity," however, these equivocations are useful. They suggest the possibility of enlarging the scope of Richards' theory by showing that different sorts of poetry have important basic similarities. This is what I shall do later in this chapter.

The other two phases of Richards' multiple meaning theory, approach and outcome, are affected by the apparently limited scope of his account of the activity of reading poetry. Every stage in Richards' account of the approach to the poem—the reader's "choosing" the poem, his seeing it as alive, his adherence to surface conformities—is based on imaginative reading. What, then, about the fanciful poem, which, far from demanding such reading, seems in fact to reject it? In this connection it is interesting to note that Richards posits a range of attitudes which the reader should adopt toward the words of a poem, sometimes (as with Keats, for instance) projecting all their meaning into them; at other times (with Pope, for instance) being aware of a difference between the words and their meanings. He further speculates that imaginative poetry will usually be read projectively; fanciful poetry non-projectively.[14] There seems to be the implication here that the Vulgar Packaging View does, in the end, accurately characterize the approach to some poems. The narrowness infects the outcome of reading poetry as well. Without the concern and absorption in purpose characteristic of imaginative reading, poetry could not have the instrumental value which Richards attributes to it.

Richards himself, then, provides strong arguments against the comprehensiveness of his theory. Nonetheless, these arguments are so often included as afterthoughts, and so often forgotten as he goes on to talk about "poetry," that it has seemed

14. *Coleridge,* pp. 107–08, 110–11.

appropriate to portray him as developing a monistic literary theory, and to criticize him for its limited range of applicability.

It is not difficult to suggest remedies for the specific criticisms I have raised. Richards' exaggeration of the instrumental value of poetry can be corrected simply by tempering his claims for poetry and recognizing the other important bases of morality and science. In this way the instrumental aspect may be accepted, but placed in its proper perspective.

Richards' theory of criticism does need emendation, but the lines along which it should be developed are quite clearly indicated. To Richards' picture of the evaluation of the private poem by the reader's choice, we must add a theory of the evaluation of the public poem by the critic. This theory must be supplemented by a discussion of the role of the critic's pronouncements concerning the meaning of the poem. In general, the critic's evaluation of the poem should be taken as a *prediction* of the private value that will be experienced in the individual reading of the poem. This general statement must be qualified in three important ways. First, the critic's statements are usually directed to an audience of more than one person. His evaluations are, then, predictions of the private values that will be experienced in reading by a majority of that audience, not necessarily by every member. Second, the predictions are usually coupled with descriptions of the work which are best understood as complex directions concerning the way in which the poem should be approached to yield the value indicated. Thus, the critic does not simply claim that a poem is good, but that it is good because of the development of its images, or because of its delicacy. Third, the critic's evaluations usually function in a persuasive, as well as in a descriptive, fashion. He does not merely predict what taste will be; he shapes taste as well. It is this third characteristic of critical utterances which makes the relationship between the evaluation by critic and reader so complex. On the negative side, the persuasive power of the critic's statements may force an insincere response from the reader. Nonetheless, this aspect of criticism appears to be essential to the development of good taste, for the reader must frequently be shocked out of settled acceptances and rejections and forced to become acclimated to material that he "sincerely" would choose. The test of value is not an immediate reaction, but a considered one.[15] A theory of critical evaluation developed along these lines would not conflict in any obvious way with Richards' theory of choice. It is true that in his earlier works, Richards emphasizes the dangers of an unwary adherence to critical standards and the necessity for individual evaluation. But it is also obvious that Richards feels that the individual needs a tremendous amount of assistance to arrive at his own real decisions.

I have suggested that critical evaluations are frequently coupled with critical descriptions suggesting approaches to the poem. Although the adoption of these different approaches is central to Richards' critical theory, we do not find in Richards' writings any analysis of the ways in which the reader comes by these approaches. There is a tremendous range of effective ways in which the reader may be led to the poem, but it is possible to discriminate two major avenues. First, there is the selective emphasis on facets of the structure or materials of the work, embodied in statements, for instance, about its imagery or rhythmic scheme. Second, there is characterization of the total effect of the work, embodied in statements, for example, about its stridency or delicacy. In the first instance, the reader is *pushed* toward an adequate interpretation by his concentra-

15. Cf. Henry D. Aiken, "A Pluralistic Analysis of Aesthetic Value," *Philosophical Review, 59* (1950), 493–513.

tion on selected features of the work; in the second he is *pulled* toward an adequate interpretation by projection of an end effect to be achieved.[16] Again, there seems to be nothing in these speculations concerning the function of critical descriptions which conflicts with Richards' critical theory. Indeed, some such account of their function seems to be demanded by his theory.

These suggestions concerning the function of critical statements obviously need to be further tailored to Richards' theory. Thus Richards' requirement of multiple approaches to the poem will have important effects upon the criteria of adequacy of criticism and the precise relationship between evaluation by critic and reader. Though I shall not attempt to work out these details here, I do not envisage serious difficulties in doing so. In this way, then, by expansion of his critical theory, we can avoid the second specific difficulty I raised concerning Richards literary theory.

The serious general criticism that the theory is too narrow has two parts: first, the theory seems to be applicable only to poetic literary works; second, it seems to be applicable only to a limited range of what is usually considered to be poetry. The first difficulty is easier to overcome than the second. It is clear that Richards typically thinks of rhymed verse when he depicts the nature of literature. Indeed, he is as well known for his analyses of the inseparability of rhythm and rhyme from the meanings of the words of a poem as for any other aspect of his work. In *Coleridge,* as we saw, he refers to meter as a "movement of meanings."[17] Nevertheless, there is ample precedent in Richards for interpreting his use of the word "poetry" to refer

16. Cf. Arnold Isenberg, "Critical Communication," *Philosophical Review, 58* (1949), 330–44; Frank Sibley, "Aesthetic Concepts," *Philosophical Review, 68* (1959), 442–50.

17. Ch. 5; see also *Principles,* ch. 17; *Practical Criticism,* pt. 3, ch. 4.

more generally to literary works of art. At one place or another he identifies the following works as poetry: *Paradise Lost, The Divine Comedy, The Pilgrim's Progress, King Lear,* and the *New Testament.*[18] Furthermore, he calls Rabelais, Swift, Voltaire, and Henry James "poets."[19] Richards prefers to cite examples of verse to illustrate his views because he feels that its greater complexity—due to its rhythm and rhyme—provides simpler and more telling illustrations of his points than does any other form of literature. The only difference, he explains in *Principles,* between the reading of a poem and "other literary experiences" is the "greater simplicity" of the latter (p. 117). In *Coleridge,* he remarks:

> For convenience I have taken, as examples of Fancy and Imagination, short passages of a few lines only. But the contrast might be illustrated equally with whole works. Thus, in prose fiction, . . . any presentation of an integral view of life will take the structure of Imagination. The units imaginatively disposed may themselves be products of Fancy; and, conversely, a series of imaginative passages may be arranged (as beads on a string) in the mode of Fancy—a structure characteristic of Hardy. (p. 95)

At one point he even acknowledges the greater complexity of some experiences of non-poetic literary works: the fullest imaginative experiences are those of tragedy, rivaled solely by the "attitudes of Falstaff and the Voltaire of *Candide.*"[20] The only place where Richards emphasizes the differences between different literary forms is in the last chapter of *Coleridge,* where

18. See *Principles,* pp. 30, 75; *Science and Poetry,* p. 72; *Practical Criticism,* p. 271.
19. *Principles,* pp. 76, 213.
20. Ibid., p. 247.

he contrasts the potentialities of modern poetry with the dis-
solution of consciousness evident in the modern novel. But
even here his complaint is not with the form of the novel, but
with the current use of this form. He contrasts it with much
more "prosaic" *Tom Jones: "Tom Jones,* of course, is not a
poem; but the components which enter into its prose-fabric
and give it its power are of kinds which do not enter into
Jacob's Room or *Ulysses;* and, otherwise disposed and inter-
related, they are more essential parts of the structure of great
poetry than those which do" (p. 225). The obvious trouble with
the modern novel is not that it is prose, but that it is not imaginative.

More important than Richards' use of the word "poetry" or
his discussions of particular works, however, is the fact that his
theory is eminently applicable to what is usually considered
to be prose. In "Poetry as an Instrument of Research,"
Richards emphasizes that his definition of poetry as fluid, non-
assertive language is a "technical" one.[21] This is not, I would
suggest, because such language is uncharacteristic of verse (it
is a "use of words . . . very frequent . . . in poetry"[22]), but
rather because it may characterize some prose as well. The contrast between prose and poetry which he draws in this essay is
the contrast between assertive and non-assertive language.
There is no reason why literary prose works cannot be non-
assertive, living organisms which demand a multiple interpretation. And given Richards' analysis of metaphor, the fact
that metaphoric relationships (between characters, plots, and
settings) are central features of much literary prose explains
how prose may have this non-assertive status.

The theory, then, cuts across traditional distinctions between
poetry and prose. But it still seems to be too restrictive in scope,

21. *Speculative Instruments,* pp. 149, 150.
22. Ibid., p. 148.

for it does not appear to cover fanciful literature. There are two possibilities: On the one hand, we might simply accept the narrowness of Richards' theory, recognize that it is applicable only to certain literary works, but argue that it nevertheless has value; on the other hand, we might try to claim that the theory is applicable to all literary works. Unfortunately, the first suggestion demands the development of a second theory to identify those works to which the first theory is applicable; the second suggestion runs counter to our experience with literature. There does seem to be a solution to the basic problem, however, which avoids the difficulties arising from each of the suggested remedies. It is to combine the two approaches in such a way that their advantages are compounded and their disadvantages eliminated.

The key to this solution lies in our recognizing the wide scope of the approach to the literary work as a living thing. Not only should we view imaginative literary works as living organisms, but we should view *every* literary work as a living organism. This attitude always demands, as it did in Richards' analysis of the imaginative poem, an active approach to the work in which the reader attempts to look at it from as many different perspectives as possible.

It is tempting to suggest that the active approach is demanded not only by literature, but by works of fine art as well. The familiar observations that the work of art has an "intrinsic" value, and that it is valued, "in and for itself," may simply reflect the respect for the work which is at the heart of this approach. George Santayana's "radically absurd and contradictory"[23] "objectification" of pleasure as the differential of true aesthetic appreciation seems relevant here. As with Richards' "projection" of meanings into the words of the poem,

23. George Santayana, *The Sense of Beauty* (New York, 1896), p. 45.

this objectification may actually represent a way of *approaching* the work of art, not an account of the ontological status of our feelings. The development of these suggestions concerning non-literary works of art is not directly relevant to my concern here, but their plausibility supports my claim that the extension of Richards' theory of imaginative poetry to all literary works of art may lie in the common approach demanded by all these works.

The multiple approach to the literary work of art, we have seen, leads to its multiple interpretation and the attempt to interrelate the resulting interpretations. At this point there first appears the major divergence between the expriences of different sorts of literary works. If the work is an imaginative one, the attempts to interrelate its different interpretations yield the peculiar values of imaginative poetry outlined above. The pitting of interpretation against interpretation involves the reader in the positing and balancing of frameworks of interpretation, and thus involves him indirectly with the balancing of their associated purposes. But the attempt to relate the different interpretations may yield quite different results. Richards himself sometimes describes the situation. In *Coleridge,* he notes this difference between imagination and fancy: In imagination "all the possible characters of any part are elicited and a place found for them," though "if enough of the possibilities of the part-meanings come in we overlook any that must stay out. With Fancy, we . . . 'overlook' them in quite another sense, we voluntarily and expressly ignore them. . . . We just ignore what is discrepant, as when we see pictures in the fire or shapes in the clouds" (p. 92). In *Rhetoric,* he stresses the important effects on the meaning of a passage of "words . . . which we might have used instead, and, together with these, the reasons why we did not use them. Another such extension looks to the other uses, in other contexts, of what we, too simply, call 'the same word.' The meaning of a word on some occasions is quite as much in what it keeps out, or at a distance, as in what it brings in" (p. 63).

These passages suggest a radically different, non-imaginative way in which the reader's experience of a work might develop. In this experience, the pitting of interpretation against interpretation does not lead to the *inclusion* and consequent balancing of meanings and interpretive frameworks that imaginative reading does. Instead, it leads to the *exclusion* of all but one or a few of these meanings and frameworks. In *Principles,* as I have noted, Richards explicitly associates two sorts of poetry with the "two ways in which impulses may be organized; by exclusion and by inclusion, by synthesis and by elimination" (p. 249). Such poems as "Ode to the Nightingale" and "Sir Patrick Spens" fall in the group which yields a synthesis of impulses through inclusion; "Rose Aylmer" and "Love's Philosophy" fall in the group which yields experiences characterized by the elimination of impulses. We can use Richards' terminology to distinguish the two sorts of literature. Literature which yields imaginative, inclusive experiences is "inclusive"; literature which yields non-imaginative, exclusive experiences is "exclusive."

It is important to contrast the non-imaginative interpretation of exclusive literature with the "literal" interpretation of factual utterance. The two sorts of interpretation are similar in their end results. Both exclusive literature and factual utterance have single meanings. In this respect, they are different from inclusive literature, which carries a multiplicity of meanings for imaginative interpretation. Nevertheless, there is an important difference between the literal interpretation of factual utterance and the non-imaginative interpretation of exclusive literature. In literal interpretation, the reader, as Richards remarks in *Rhetoric,* "guesses" at an interpretation of a factual utterance (p. 55), accepting it if it is workable. In non-imaginative interpretation, on the contrary, the reader establishes an interpretation of exclusive literature through careful exclusion of all irrelevant interpretations. The difference between the two sorts of interpretation can be characterized as a difference between the development of a working hypothesis, for factual utterance, and the establishment of a truth through exclusion of all alternatives but one, for exclusive literature.

This difference between literal and non-imaginative interpretation highlights an important similarity between imaginative and non-imaginative interpretation of literature. As noted above, imaginative and non-imaginative interpretation differ in their products: exclusive literature has one primary meaning; inclusive literature has several meanings, no single one of which is most important. Nevertheless, in both imaginative and non-imaginative interpretation, the reader's attention is focused not upon what is said but upon the process of interpretation. In this respect they differ from the literal interpretation of factual utterances, which places primary stress on what is said. In imaginative interpretation the reader becomes absorbed in balancing the frameworks which give rise to the different meanings he discovers. In non-imaginative reading he becomes absorbed in excluding certain meanings and interpretive frameworks as irrelevant. This concern with the process of interpretation rather than its product stems from the reader's approach to the work of literature as a living organism. It indicates the similarities of the intrinsic values of the two sorts of experience. The non-imaginative reading of exclusive literature, no less than the imaginative reading of inclusive literature, involves the reader with the purposes underlying interpretive frameworks. Literal interpretation of factual utterance does not.

These differences and similarities show how the scope of

Richards' theory can be enlarged. In having equally central multiple meanings, inclusive literature differs from exclusive literature, which has only one basic meaning. But the similarities in their modes of interpretation and in their intrinsic values allow them both to be characterized as "literature."

Although I have used some passages from Richards to develop the distinction between the imaginative and non-imaginative literary experience, I cannot claim that he himself envisages this solution to the criticism that his theory is too narrow. In the course of the passage from *Coleridge* quoted above, he notes that "letting an awareness of [the] . . . *irrelevance* in" of certain part-meanings is an example of "a special complex use of Fancy, not to be mistaken for the norm" (p. 92). (He cites burlesque as an example here.) In "The Future of Poetry" he seems to envisage some poetry as being valued primarily for its translatable "precipitate."[24] I can only suggest that, had Richards never lost sight of his important distinction between the process and product of reading, he might have realized that the irrelevance "let in" in interpretation does not necessarily figure in the product of interpretation but may be important to its process, and that the fact that an utterance is translatable does not mean that its value lies in what it says.

I would use this distinction between the product and process of interpretation to answer the final lingering criticism by the average critic of Chapter 1. This is that Richards, even in his multiple meaning theory, ignores the importance of considerations of truth in poetry. The feeling that considerations of truth are important in poetry results, I would say, from the critic's confusion of exclusive literature with factual utterances. Interpretation of such literature yields products as true or false as does that of factual utterance, but the value of exclusive lit-

24. *Screens,* p. 123.

erature lies not in these products, but in the process of interpretation. Thus considerations of truth are unimportant.[25]

Only one obstacle stands in the way of my solution to the
problem of the narrowness of Richards' theory of literature.
This is his suggestion that fanciful poetry is frequently read
non-projectively, which, if true, would mean that it should not
be approached as if it were a living organism. Here I can do
nothing more than point out again that Richards equivocates
on this matter, and add that my interpretation transforms a
theory seriously hampered by its limited scope into one which
illuminates all sorts of literature. Indeed, with its unified and
coherent treatment of the central problems raised by the entire
range of literature for reader, critic, moralist, and aesthetician,
Richards' theory of literature emerges as one not only im-
mensely helpful to those puzzled about literature, but also
highly suggestive to those searching for a general theory of
aesthetics.

25. See Jerome Schiller, "An Alternative to 'Aesthetic Disinterestedness,' " *Journal of Aesthetics and Art Criticism, 22* (1964), 298–301.

Appendix 1:
Hotopf's Criticism of Richards

Despite the comprehensiveness of W. H. N. Hotopf's *Language, Thought, and Comprehension, A Case Study of the Writings of I. A. Richards* (Bloomington, Indiana University Press, 1965), its orientation is so different from mine that there is little overlapping of ideas. Hotopf professes two major reasons for his concern with Richards' works: an interest in theories about the influence of language on thought, and a concern with failure of communication (p. 1). He develops these concerns through an exhaustive analysis of Richards' theory of comprehension, a study of the misunderstandings of Richards' writings, a discussion of Richards' errors in terms of Richards' own theories about the linguistic sources of error, and a reconsideration of these errors in terms of Richards' attitudes toward the self and its relation to others (p. 7). As might be suspected from this list, Hotopf has his own axes to grind, and a good part of the book is devoted to attacks on contemporary philosophic movements such as linguistic analysis, as well as to criticism of Richards' theories. In order to review as exhaustively as he does the mistakes in Richards' thought and the misunderstandings of those who have written about him, Hotopf finds it necessary to summarize Richards' major writings from *The Meaning of Meaning* to *How To Read a Page* in four very detailed chapters. Hotopf does not, however, develop Richards' theory of literature in the course of his discussion. To some extent this can be explained by Hotopf's purposes. He says that he is concerned with

169

Appendix 1

Principles, Science and Poetry, and *Practical Criticism* "not funda-
mentally because of their contribution to literary criticism as a
specialist subject, but because the theory of value worked out in
them underlies Richards' teaching activities" (p. 34).

Hotopf also believes that Richards abandons a consideration of
poetry for that of non-poetic language in the later works, though
he admits that the model for comprehension is set in Richards' discussion of poetry (pp. 34, 90), and that Richards' concern in all his
works was "with communication rather than with literary criticism" (p. 211). Hotopf, then, does not consider in detail some of
Richards' works which are centrally concerned with poetry, such
as "Interactions of Words," "Poetry as an Instrument of Research," the "Proem" to *Goodbye Earth,* and "The Future of
Poetry." Thus, in many ways, Hotopf has taken a tack directly opposed to my own. He claims that all of Richards' writings—including those ostensibly concerned with poetry—really illuminate
Richards' views on communication and the relationship between
language and thought, while I have suggested that in many passages where Richards seems to be talking about non-poetic themes,
he is really talking about poetry. I defend my approach by emphasizing a point which Hotopf himself acknowledges: many of
Richards' later views concerning non-poetic language are modeled
after his earlier views concerning poetry. For instance, Hotopf
notes that Richards' ideas on grammar in *Interpretation in Teaching* suggest "the attitude to reading that comes from poetry"
(p. 121). A few pages earlier Hotopf notes of Richards that "in
all his psychologizing about perception, thinking, and feeling in
their general aspects, one feels the want of detailed, intensive experiencing, in contrast, for instance, to what he says about poetry"
(p. 109). Elsewhere Hotopf states that Richards' search for multiple
meanings in passages from Aristotle and Whitehead does not "re-
veal anything commensurate to the few examples he takes from
Shakespeare" (p. 254). Hotopf clearly suggests, then, that Richards'
discussion of poetry is significant. Thus, even Hotopf provides
some support for my substantive arguments that poetry is Richards'
deepest concern, and that his other discussions can be viewed as,
in large part, secondary.

So far as specific details of Richards' aesthetic theory are concerned, however, the book is not very helpful. There is, for instance, no discussion of the communicative theory of the early

170

works and no detailed analysis of the non-assertive quality of poetic discourse. But again, Hotopf's interpretations of the two senses of "emotive" language (pp. 28 ff.), of the ambiguity in "impulse" (pp. 43 ff.), and of the similarity of poetry and philosophy (p. 134) seem to support some of my claims. On the other hand, he views most of the features of *Coleridge* which I find centrally important—such as the imagination, the fact of mind, the fusions of parts and of words and meanings in the imaginative experience, and the stress on the process of utterance—as evidence of Richards' concern with the unconscious and an anti-rational, mystical streak in his thinking (ch. 4).

I believe that Hotopf goes to Richards for precisely those things which Richards can least well provide him, theories of meaning and value. It is not surprising, then, that Hotopf finds so many difficulties in these theories. It is beyond my purpose to comment in detail on the adequacy of Hotopf's criticisms. Many of his comments are very telling indeed. Some, particularly those stemming from his anti-individualistic bias, are not. As the argument of my book shows, I believe that Hotopf's interpretation is based upon a misreading of Richards' discussions of meaning and an overemphasis on his discussions of value. Nevertheless, I believe that his book is of value to students of Richards. Hotopf's critical summaries of much of the available secondary writing on Richards make his study important for anyone interested in further investigating these facets of Richards' thought. I recommend it as an interpretation very different from and basically opposed to my own.

Appendix 2:
Richards' *So Much Nearer*

My study of I. A. Richards' theory of literature had been completed at the time of the appearance of *So Much Nearer: Essays Toward a World English* (Harcourt, Brace & World, Inc., New York, 1968). Some of the essays in this work, most importantly "The Future of Poetry," had been available to me earlier; some, such as "Toward a World English," which is his latest apology for Basic English, are not relevant to my subject. Nevertheless, it seems appropriate to try to indicate the relationship of some of the themes developed in this latest book with Richards' theory as found in the earlier works. Doubtless, by the time this study appears in print, Richards will have published other relevant materials. I can only say that I hope he does so, though it will render my work incomplete.

At some points in this latest work, Richards underscores the importance of earlier themes which we have seen to be central to his thought. Thus he notes that his "set of suggestions" concerning meaning in "Toward a Theory of Comprehending" is "by far the most enterprising speculative instrument I have been concerned to design" (p. 63), one which, though largely neglected by his critics, entirely supercedes earlier discussions such as those in *Practical Criticism* (p. 64). He insists at several points on the importance of proper *sequencing* in the development of language skills (pp. 7–8, 38–40, 59). Occasionally old themes appear in a new guise, as, for example, when the sort of interference with adequate interpretation which Richards traces to "doctrinal adhesions" in *Practical Criticism* is pictured as stemming from "intervening meanings" (pp. xi, 123–27).

Richards frequently touches on topics which are central to what I have called his multiple meaning theory. In this connection I might note his relating of meaning and choice (p. 148); his distinction between treating an utterance (in this case a dictionary entry) as a process and as an outcome (p. 98); his insistence on the need for taking account of soul in developing a theory of language (pp. 92–93); his depiction of divergent frameworks underlying utterances—"Mencius through the Looking-Glass" (pp. 201–17) and "Sources of World Conflict" (pp. 218–39) which rely heavily on *Mencius on the Mind* and *Basic in Teaching: East and West,* respectively; and his stress on the *mediating* function of meanings (p. 130).

Richards emphasizes two new themes in this book: the systematic nature of language and the greater importance of practice than theory. In Chapter 4 of my study, I show, in support of my suggestion that Richards finds it essential to regard the poem as a living thing, how he likens language to a society (see above, p. 109). Throughout *So Much Nearer,* the parallel between language and a society is stressed, but the aim is somewhat different. Language is here viewed as being similar to a society in that it is organized in accordance with flexible rules in such a way that its "health" (its proper understanding) is based upon free give-and-take among its elements. The theme is most clearly developed in "Meanings Anew," and it is in this essay that we find the clue to how this new theme should be related to themes developed in Richards' earlier writings. The reason for viewing language as a system modeled on a society is to understand how the *exclusion* of meanings comes about: "In the normal case, the unit of utterance will be a sentence. The one or more words in it will participate in its work in ways which usually entail the subordination or sacrifice of their other possibilities to its purposes. . . . In all this, each part . . . has a double task: to *combine* with the rest in the over-all undertaking and to *exclude* whatever is not contributory to it" (p. 119).

These new pronouncements concerning language must be seen, then, as attempts on Richards' part to clarify his earlier descriptions of the way in which superfluity of meanings is excluded in comprehending utterances. It will be remembered that in his later works Richards replaced the older mechanistic view of specification of meanings by one in which the activity of the reader was stressed (see above, pp. 69–73). In this connection Richards noted the flexibility required to fit the meanings of the parts to a projected meaning of the whole. In his latest book, while acknowledging the exploratory nature of comprehension (p. 116), he stresses rather the *system* which controls the operation of the feedforward and feedback involved in comprehension. When Richards speaks, therefore, about the cooperation between systems to yield meanings (pp. 4, 7–8, 10, 71), the interplay between elements of language (pp. 99–102, 117, 134–35, 161–63), and the need for viewing language and its meanings as a public system (pp. 10, 131, 140–41, 167–68, 195, 198), he is not altering his earlier views about language and poetry; he is merely specifying in greater detail how meanings are developed. I must confess that I do not find his analyses very illuminating. In the end, he appeals—in the analogy he draws between understanding and walking—to the facts that we learn *how* to engage in these activities without fully understanding the processes and that the situations are extremely complex (pp. 135–39). But, despite the fact that this new theme needs much fuller development, it does not undermine in any way the multiple meaning theory, but merely attempts to provide additional material for its understanding.

The second new theme which I noted above does seem to me to represent a shift in Richards' views. Richards' impatience with theory, his emphasis on the immediately effective, is reflected in the change in tone in some of these later pieces. The questioning, tentative tone of the essays of *Speculative Instruments* is replaced in such essays as "Some Glances at Current Linguistics" by a directness approaching that of *The Meaning of Meaning* or *Principles*. Not all the essays—certainly not "The Future of Poetry"—exhibit this change, but Richards' reiteration of the theme that the urgent need for immediate solutions to practical problems vitiates much contemporary speculation is frequent enough (pp. 15–16, 68–69, 83, 204) to make us wonder whether he has abandoned his appreciation of the subtle value of philosophy shown in *Speculative Instruments*. I would hesitate to come to this conclusion. Rather, I feel, we find here an appreciation on Richards' part of his overstatement of the value of philosophy (or poetry), for which I have criticized even his multiple meaning theory. I do not find Richards' impatience in *So Much Nearer* very much more attractive than his hesitancy in *Speculative Instruments*. Taken together, however, they show us Richards' sensitivity to these issues concerning theory and practice. Let us hope that he will provide us with a good deal more material on this theme.

Bibliography

I. I. A. Richards' Works

A. Books

Basic in Teaching, East and West, London, Kegan Paul, 1935.
Basic Rules of Reason, London, Kegan Paul, 1933.
Coleridge on Imagination, New York, Harcourt, Brace, 1935.
The Foundations of Aesthetics (with C. K. Ogden and James Wood), London, George Allen and Unwin, 1922.
Goodbye Earth and Other Poems, New York, Harcourt, Brace, 1958.
How To Read a Page, A Course in Efficient Reading with an Introduction to a Hundred Great Words, New York, W. W. Norton, 1942 (paperback edition, Boston, Beacon Press, 1958).
Interpretation in Teaching, London, Kegan Paul, 1938.
The Meaning of Meaning, A Study of the Influence of Language upon Thought and of the Science of Symbolism (with C. K. Ogden), London, Kegan Paul, 1923.
Mencius on the Mind, Experiments in Multiple Definition, London, Kegan Paul, 1932.
Nations and Peace, New York, Simon and Schuster, 1947.
The Philosophy of Rhetoric, The Mary Flexner Lectures on the Humanities, III, New York, Oxford University Press, 1936.
Practical Criticism, A Study of Literary Judgment, London, Kegan Paul, 1929.

Bibliography

Principles of Literary Criticism, New York, Harcourt, Brace, 1924 (third edition, 1928).
Science and Poetry, New York, W. W. Norton, 1926 (second edition, London, Kegan Paul, 1935).
The Screens and Other Poems, New York, Harcourt, Brace, 1960.
So Much Nearer, Essays toward a World English, New York, Harcourt, Brace & World, 1968.
Speculative Instruments, Chicago, University of Chicago Press, 1955.

B. Articles

"The Changing American Mind," *Harper's Magazine, 154* (1927), 239–45.
"Coleridge: The Vulnerable Poet," *Yale Review, 48* (1959), 491–504.
"Dependence of Thought on its Milieu," *Speculative Instruments,* pp. 170–78.
"Emotive Language Still," *Yale Review, 39* (1949), 108–18.
"Emotive Meaning Again," A Symposium on Emotive Meaning, *Philosophical Review, 57* (1948), 145–57. Also in *Speculative Instruments,* pp. 39–56.
"Foreword," *Speculative Instruments,* pp. ix–xii.
"The Future of the Humanities in General Education," *Journal of General Education, 1* (1947), 232–37. Also in *Speculative Instruments,* pp. 57–67.
"The Future of Poetry," *The Screens and Other Poems,* pp. 105–27. Also appears, with notes, in *So Much Nearer,* pp. 150–82.
"Fifteen Lines from Landor," *Criterion, 12* (1933), 355–70. Also in *Speculative Instruments,* pp. 181–97.
"From Criticism to Creation," *Times Literary Supplement, 3300* (May 27, 1965), 438–39. Also appears, with additions and notes, in *So Much Nearer,* pp. 3–33.
"General Education in the Humanities," *Speculative Instruments,* pp. 129–32.
"Gerard Hopkins," *Dial, 81* (1926), 195–203.
"God of Dostoievsky," *Forum, 78* (1927), 88–97.
"How Does a Poem Know When It is Finished?" *Parts and Wholes,* ed. Daniel Lerner, New York, The Free Press of Glencoe, 1963.

178

"The Idea of a University," *Speculative Instruments,* pp. 107–12.

"The Interactions of Words," *The Language of Poetry,* The *Mesures* Series in Literary Criticism, ed. Allen Tate, Princeton, Princeton University Press, 1942, pp. 65-87.

"Interpretation," *Yale Review, 32* (1943), 693-705. Also appears as "Towards Practice in Interpretation," in *Speculative Instruments,* pp. 78–90.

"Introduction," Plato's *Republic,* ed. and trans. I. A. Richards, Cambridge, Cambridge University Press, 1966, pp. 1–13.

"Introduction," *The Portable Coleridge,* ed. and intro. I. A. Richards, New York, Viking Press, 1950, pp. 1–55.

"Introduction," *Semantics, The Nature of Words and Their Meanings,* Hugh R. Walpole, New York, W. W. Norton, 1941, pp. 11–19.

"Language and Value," *Speculative Instruments,* pp. 137–45.

"Lure of High Mountaineering," *Atlantic, 139* (1927), 51–57.

"Meanings Anew," *So Much Nearer,* pp. 113–49.

"Mencius through the Looking-Glass," *So Much Nearer,* pp. 201–17. (Quotes extensively from *Mencius on the Mind.*)

"Multiple Definition," *Proceedings* of the Aristotelian Society, *34* (1933), 31–50.

"Nineteen Hundred and Now," *Atlantic, 140* (1927), 311–17.

"Notes on a Definition of Culture," *Partisan Review, 10* (1944), 310–12. Also, appears as "Education and Culture" in *Speculative Instruments,* pp. 68–71.

"Notes toward an Agreement between Literary Criticism and Some of the Sciences," *Confluence, 3* (1954), 41–56. Also in *Speculative Instruments,* pp. 3–16.

"On TSE," *Sewanee Review, 74* (1966), 21–30.

"Passage to Forster," *Forum, 78* (1927), 914–20.

"Places and the Figures," *Kenyon Review, 11* (1949), 17–30. Also in *Speculative Instruments,* pp. 155–69.

"Poetic Process and Literary Analysis," *Style in Language,* ed. Thomas A. Sebeok, Cambridge, Mass., M. I. T. Press, 1960, pp. 9–23.

"Poetry as an Instrument of Research," *Speculative Instruments,* pp. 146–54.

"Poetry of T. S. Eliot," *Living Age, 329* (1926), 112–15.

"Practice of Interpretation," *Criterion, 10* (1931), 412–20.

"Proem," *Goodbye Earth and Other Poems,* New York, Harcourt, Brace, 1958, pp. vii–x.

"Queries," *Speculative Instruments,* pp. 133–36.

"The Resourcefulness of Words," *Furioso, 1* (1941), 83–90. Also in *Speculative Instruments,* pp. 72–77.

"Responsibilities in the Teaching of English," *Essays and Studies* (English Association, London), *32* (1947), 7–20. Also in *Speculative Instruments,* pp. 91–106.

"The Secret of 'Feedforward,'" *Saturday Review of Literature* (Feb. 3, 1968), pp. 14–17.

"The Sense of Poetry: Shakespeare's 'The Phoenix and the Turtle,'" *Daedelus, 87* (Summer 1958), 86–94.

"Sentimentality," *Forum, 76* (1926), 384–91.

"Some Glances at Current Linguistics," *So Much Nearer,* pp. 65–112. Also appears, in part, as "Growing Pains" in *New York Review of Books* (April 14, 1966), pp. 20–24; in part, as "Why Generative Grammar Does Not Help" in *English Language Teaching, 22* (October 1967 and January 1968).

"Sources of Conflict," *So Much Nearer,* pp. 218–39. (Quotes extensively from *Basic in Teaching, East and West.*)

"Toward a More Synoptic View," *Speculative Instruments,* pp. 113–26.

"Towards a Theory of Translating," *Studies in Chinese Thought,* ed. Arthur F. Wright, Chicago, University of Chicago Press, 1953, pp. 247–62. Also appears as "Towards a Theory of Comprehending," in *Speculative Instruments,* pp. 17–38.

"*Troilus and Cressida* and Plato," *Hudson Review, 1* (1949), pp. 362–76. Also in *Speculative Instruments,* pp. 198–213.

"Variant Readings and Misreading," *Style in Language,* ed. Thomas A. Sebeok, Cambridge, Mass., M. I. T. Press, 1960, pp. 241–52. Also appears, with notes, in *So Much Nearer,* pp. 183–200.

"What Is Belief?" *Nation, 139* (1934), 71–74.

II.   Writings on Richards

A.   Books

Bilsky, Manuel, *The Aesthetic Theory of I. A. Richards,* unpublished Ph.D. dissertation, University of Michigan, 1951.

Eastman, Max, *Enjoyment of Poetry,* New York, Charles Scribner's Sons, 1913.

————, *The Literary Mind,* New York, Charles Scribner's Sons, 1932.

Eliot, T. S., *Selected Essays,* new ed. New York, Harcourt, Brace, 1950.

————, *The Use of Poetry and the Use of Criticism,* London, Faber & Faber, 1933.

Empson, William, *The Structure of Complex Words,* London, Chatto & Windus, 1952.

Foster, R. J., *The New Romantics,* Bloomington, Indiana University Press, 1962.

Fry, Roger, *Transformations,* Garden City, Anchor Books, 1956.

Guth, Hans P. H., *Threat as the Basis of Beauty: Pragmatist Elements in the Aesthetics of Richards, Dewey, and Burke,* unpublished Ph.D. dissertation, University of Michigan, 1957.

Hamilton, G. Rostrevor, *Poetry and Contemplation,* Cambridge, Cambridge University Press, 1937.

Hare, R. M., *The Language of Morals,* Oxford, Oxford University Press, 1952.

Hotopf, W. H. N., *Language, Thought, and Comprehension, A Case Study in the Writings of I. A. Richards,* Bloomington, University of Indiana Press, 1965.

Hyman, Stanley Edgar, *The Armed Vision,* New York, Alfred A. Knopf, 1952.

James, D. G., *Scepticism and Poetry,* London, G. Allen and Unwin, 1937.

Joseph, H. W. B., *Essays in Ancient and Modern Philosophy,* Oxford, Oxford University Press, 1935.

Krieger, Murray, *The New Apologists for Poetry,* Minneapolis, University of Minnesota Press, 1956.

Pottle, Frederick A., *The Idiom of Poetry,* Ithaca, Cornell University Press, 1946.

Ransom, John Crowe, *The New Criticism,* Norfolk, New Directions Press, 1942.

Righter, William, *Logic and Criticism,* New York, Chilmark Press, 1963.

Rudolph, Gerald Allen, *The Affective Criticism of I. A. Richards,* unpublished Ph.D. dissertation, University of Washington, 1959.

Santayana, George, *The Sense of Beauty*, New York, Charles Scribner's Sons, 1896.

Schiller, Jerome P., *I. A. Richards and the Autonomy and Personal Relevance of Poetry*, unpublished Ph. D. dissertation, Harvard University, 1960.

Stevenson, Charles L., *Ethics and Language*, New Haven, Yale University Press, 1944.

Stolnitz, Jerome, *Aesthetics and the Philosophy of Art Criticism*, Boston, Houghton Mifflin, 1960.

Tate, Allen, *On the Limits of Poetry, Selected Essays*, New York, Swallow Press & Wm. Morrow, 1948.

Tolstoy, Leo, *What Is Art? and Essays on Art*, trans. Alymer Maude, London, Oxford University Press, 1955 (first app. 1898).

West, Alick, *Crisis and Criticism*, London, Lawrence and Wishart, 1937.

Wimsatt, W. K., Jr. (with Monroe C. Beardsley), *The Verbal Icon, Studies in the Meaning of Poetry*, University of Kentucky, University of Kentucky Press, 1954.

Wimsatt, W. K., Jr. and Cleanth Brooks, *Literary Criticism, A Short History*, New York, Alfred A. Knopf, 1957.

B. Articles

Abrams, M. H., "Belief and the Suspension of Disbelief," *Literature and Belief*, English Institute Essays, 1957, ed. M. H. Abrams, New York, Columbia University Press, 1958, pp. 1–30.

Aiken, C. P., "A Scientific Approach to Criticism," *Nation and Athenaeum, 36* (1925), 585–86.

Aiken, Henry D., "A Pluralistic Analysis of Aesthetic Value," *Philosophical Review, 59* (1950), 493–513.

Belgion, Montgomery, "What Is Criticism?" *Criterion, 10* (1930), 118–39.

Bentley, Eric Russell, "The Early I. A. Richards," *Rocky Mountain Review, 8* (1944), 29–36.

Bethell, S. L., "Suggestions toward a Theory of Value," *Criterion, 14* (1935), 239–50.

Bilsky, Manuel, "I. A. Richards on Belief," *Philosophy and Phenomenological Research, 12* (1951), 105–15.

————, "I. A. Richards' Theory of Metaphor," *Modern Philology, 50* (1952), 130–37.

————, "I. A. Richards' Theory of Value," *Philosophy and Phenomenological Research, 14* (1954), 536–45.

Black, Max, "Some Objections to Ogden and Richards' Theory of Interpretation," *Journal of Philosophy, 39* (1942), 281–90.

————, "Some Questions about Emotive Meaning," A Symposium on Emotive Meaning, *Philosophical Review, 57* (1948), 111–26.

Blackmur, R. P., "San Giovanni in Venere: Allen Tate as a Man of Letters," *Sewanee Review, 67* (1959), 614–31.

Bronowski, J., review of M. Belgion, *The Human Parrot and Other Essays, Criterion, 11* (1932), 322–24.

Chisholm, Roderick, "Intentionality and the Theory of Signs," *Philosophical Studies, 3* (1952), 56–63.

Crane, R. S., "I. A. Richards on the Art of Interpretation," *Ethics, 59* (1949), 112–26.

Cruttwell, Patrick, "Second Thoughts, IV: I. A. Richards' *Practical Criticism,*" *Essays in Criticism, 8* (1958), 1–15.

Daiches, David, "The Principles of Literary Criticism," *New Republic, 98* (1939), 95–98.

Eliot, T. S., "Literature, Science and Dogma," *Dial, 82* (1927), 239–43.

————, "Religion and Literature," *Selected Essays,* New York, Harcourt, Brace, 1950, pp. 343–54.

Gentry, George, "Reference and Relation," *Journal of Philosophy, 40* (1943), 253–61.

Glicksberg, Charles I., "I. A. Richards and the Science of Criticism," *Sewanee Review, 46* (1948), 520–33.

Graff, Gerald E., "The Later Richards and the New Criticism," *Criticism, 9* (1967), 229–42.

Harding, D. W., "I. A. Richards," *Scrutiny, 1* (1933), 327–38.

Hochmuth, Marie, "I. A. Richards and the New Rhetoric," *Quarterly Journal of Speech, 44* (1958), 1–16.

Isenberg, Arnold, "Critical Communication," *Philosophical Review, 58* (1949), 330–44.

Knight, E. Helen, "Some Aesthetic Theories of Mr. Richards," *Mind, 36* (1927), 69–76.

Leavis, F. R., "Dr. Richards, Bentham and Coleridge," *Scrutiny, 3* (1935), 382–402.

McLuhan, H. M., "Poetic vs. Rhetorical Exegesis, the Case for Leavis against Richards and Empson," *Sewanee Review, 52* (1944), 266–76.

Pollock, T. C., "A Critique of I. A. Richards' Theory of Language and Literature," *A Theory of Meaning Analyzed,* General Semantics Monographs, 3, ed. M. Kending, Chicago, Institute of General Semantics, 1942, pp. 1–25.

Ransom, John Crowe, "A Psychologist Looks at Poetry," *Virginia Quarterly Review, 11* (1935), 575–92.

Rudolph, G. A., "The Aesthetic Field of I. A. Richards," *Journal of Aesthetics and Art Criticism, 14* (1956), 348–58.

Russell, Bertrand, "The Meaning of Meaning," *Dial, 81* (1926), 114–21.

Schiller, Jerome, "An Alternative to 'Aesthetic Disinterestedness,' " *Journal of Aesthetics and Art Criticism, 22* (1964), 295–302.

Sesonske, Alexander, "Truth in Art," *Journal of Philosophy, 53* (1956), 345–53.

Shanks, Edward, "An Experiment with Literature," *Saturday Review, 147* (1929), 865–66.

Sibley, Frank, "Aesthetic Concepts," *Philosophical Review, 68* (1959), 421–50.

Spaulding, J. G., "Richards' Theory of Poetic Value," *A Theory of Meaning Analyzed,* General Semantics Monographs, 3, ed. M. Kending, Chicago, Institute of General Semantics, 1942, pp. 26–35.

Twitchett, E. G., "A Vision of Judgment," *London Mercury, 20* (1929), 598–605.

Vivas, Eliseo, "Four Notes on I. A. Richards' Aesthetic Theory," *Philosophical Review, 44* (1935), 354–67.

Wellek, René, "On Rereading I. A. Richards," *The Southern Review,* n.s. *3* (1967), 533–54.

Wimsatt, W. K., Jr., "Poetry and Morals, A Relation Reargued," *The Verbal Icon,* University of Kentucky, University of Kentucky Press, 1954, pp. 85–102.

Woolf, L., "How Not to Read Poetry," *Nation and Athenaeum, 45* (1929), 538.

Index

Acceptance, 6, 120–21. *See also* Beliefs

Activity, reader's: in interpretation of all language, 69–74, 81, 86; in interpretation of poetry, 79, 81, 86, 104; in receiving communicated poem, 99–100

Aesthetician. *See* Interests in literature

Ambiguity, 78, 81. *See also* Meanings, multiple, of words

Approaches, multiple, to poem, 112–16, 159–60

Attitudes, 120, 123, 127; in impulse theory, 5 f., 56 ff., 120, 126 f.; communicated in poetry, 97; ambiguity in Richards' treatment of, 130–31, 143

Balance. *See* Equilibrium in impulse theory

Beliefs, irrelevance of, in poetry, 5–6, 120–23, 144; criticism of Richards' views on, 10

Choice: in evaluation, 28, 80, 82, 102–05, 173; among meanings,

69 f.; and correctness of reading, 111, 115–16

Chung Yung, 71, 150

Coherence, as test of correctness of reading, 113, 115

Coleridge, 18–41 passim; Richards' interpretation of, ix, 20 f.

Coleridge on Imagination: different interests in literature confused in, 35–42; as suggesting facets of Richards' theory of literature, 46, 66–67, 80, 88, 103, 118, 132–33, 140; themes from early works in, 127–28

Communication, poem as a, 5, 92–100, 105–07; and "good reader," 96–99; and evaluation, 101 f.

Completeness of poetic experience, 80, 107, 136–37

Conflict. *See* Mediation through poetry

Content versus form. *See* Form versus content

Contexts, 59–61. *See also* Meaning, context theory of

Continuity of poetry and life, 5,

185

Index

125 f.; Richards' view of, criticized, 12, 144

Correctness of reading, 5, 92, 98, 105 f., 112–16; sources of misreading, 8, 20, 32, 98, 172–73; related to value, 114–16

Critic. *See* Interests in literature

Criticism, Richards' theory of: summarized, 115–17; criticized and amended, 150–53, 158–60. *See also* Evaluation; Theory, instrumental use of

Criticisms, familiar, of Richards, 7–13, 144

"Dejection" (Coleridge), 83

Denham, Sir John, 85

Detachment, 48, 99. *See also* Impersonality

"Ecstasie" (Donne), 149 n.

Education, 7 ff., 72, 172

Emotive language, 6, 88; expressing attitudes, 51–54; arousing attitudes, 54–57; demanding a special sort of interpretation, 57–58, 73–82; in context theory of meaning, 60–61

Equilibrium in impulse theory, 5, 48, 77, 82, 125; versus action, 5, 128

Evaluation, 102–05; subjective versus objective, 103 f., 150–52, 158–59; confusion with value, 104. *See also* Criticism, Richards' theory of; Rules; Theory, instrumental use of

Experience of the poem, ambiguity in Richards' account of, 101, 104–06, 128, 143

Fact and value, realms of: characterized, 29–30, 120–22; conflict between, and resolution, 30–32, 35, 132–39

Fact of mind, 29, 32, 78–79, 116, 140. *See also* Process versus product of reading

Fallacy: affective, 13; pathetic, 109

Fancy, 23, 24–26, 154–55. *See also* Imagination

Feed-forward, 66, 73, 174

Flexibility, 73, 153–54, 174–75

Fluid language and rigid language: senses of, 63, 73–76, 114 f., 154–55; Richards' confusion of senses of, 75–76, 80–81, 86–87

Form versus content, 32, 48 f., 78, 104, 157

Frameworks: in interpretation of all language, 66–69, 72–73, 81; examples of, 67, 173; in interpretation of poetry, 79, 82

Good sense, 28; confusion in Richards' account of, 39–40, 118. *See also* Rules; Theory, instrumental use of

Growth: in meanings in reading poetry, 25 ff., 31, 80, 116; of individual in reading, 50, 81–82, 107 ff.; of individual in evaluation, 102–03, 116

Idealism, Coleridge's, 21, 22–23, 29–30

Imagination, 24–26; distinguished from fancy, 22, 26, 34; different senses of, 23 f., 29–30, 34; projective, *see* Projection

Impersonality, 98–99, 100

Impulses: in analysis of poetry, 4, 35, 92, 97, 143–44; as descriptive of all experience, 5, 55–56, 96–97, 125; criticism of Richards' views on, 11, 12–13, 56–

Index

Psychology, 4–5, 55–56; criticism of Richards' views on, 11–12. *See also* Impulses

Purposes: underlying all utterances, 64–67, 155; in reading of poetry, 79, 82, 101, 103–04, 166; in philosophy, 135–36, 138–39; in all human activities, 138–39

Reader. *See* Interests in literature

Realizing intuition, 21 f., 31, 46–47; confusions in Richards' account of, 40–42

Referential language, 6, 56, 58–60. *See also* Meaning, context theory of

Religion, 5–7, 121–24; criticism of Richards' views on, 11, 144; and poetry, 123–24

Richards, I. A.: misunderstandings of, 3, 13 f.; changes in interests of, 8–9, 14, 76, 132, 170; changes in views of, viii, 14–16; changes in tone of writings of, v–ix passim, 15 f., 35, 49, 120, 141, 174–75

Rigid language. *See* Fluid language and rigid language

Rules: in communication, 100; in correct interpretation, 115–117; and evaluation, 117. *See also* Theory, instrumental use of

Saying versus what is said. *See* Process versus product of reading

Science, 6, 121–23, 144; criticism of Richards' views on, 10–11, 144, 145–56; and poetry, 32, 123–24

Self-realization, 22, 26, 30, 79, 81 f., 103, 114

Sincerity, 96, 150–51; Tolstoy's view of, 95

Sonnet XCIV (Shakespeare), 149 n.

Stock response, 128–29

Style, Richards'. *See* Richards, I. A.

Symbolic language. *See* Referential language

Synaesthesis, 48, 77, 113, 125

Theory, instrumental use of, 21, 26, 28, 31, 34–35, 40; confusion in Richards' account of, 39–40, 141. *See also* Criticism, Richards' theory of; Rules

Theory of literature: nature of a, 42–44, 149; Richards', sketched, 44–47, 87, 116–17, 142, 146–47; Richards', its narrow scope, 150, 154–57, 160–68

Tolstoy, Leo, 93–95

Tone, Richards'. *See* Richards, I. A.

Transference of ability in poetry, 129–32, 139–40

Truth, irrelevance of, in poetry, 6, 120–23, 144, 167–68; criticism of Richards' views on, 10

Unity of poetic language, 24, 25–26, 49

Untranslatability of poetry, 78–79, 155

Value, impulse theory of, 5, 124–25, 128, 132; criticized, 11, 146, 171

Value of poetry, instrumental; 33, 120–40 passim, 144; criticism of Richards' views on, 12, 150, 158

Value of poetry, intrinsic, 5, 23,